EXPLODING THE MYTH OF SELF-DEFENSE

EXPLODING THE MYTH OF SELF-DEFENSE

A Survival Guide for Every Woman

JUDITH FEIN, PH.D.

Torrance Publishing Company
P.O. Box 2558
Sebastopol, CA 95473
(707) 823-3581

First Edition

Printed in the United States of America

Library of Congress Cataloging-in Publication Data

Fein, Judith
Exploding The Myth of Self-Defense

Includes index
1. Self-Defense for Women. 2. Rape—Prevention
3. Self-respect. 4. Women—Psychology.
I. Title
Library of Congress Catalog Card Number: 93-60018
ISBN: 0-929523-01-6

Cover Art: "Cinderella Liberty" © Nancy Worthington
Cover Design: Nancy Worthington
Jack Fisher—Communications Graphics
Editor: Jean Gilliam

This book is dedicated to my mother,
Minnie Lifschutz Fein,
in loving memory

CONTENTS

PREFACE

In 1981, in Are You A Target?, my first book on self-defense for women, I wrote: "This book is about freedom. Its purpose is to help you gain the knowledge, insights, and courage to make the necessary changes in your life to become a successful assault resister. ...You don't have to be a victim. Being a resister means that you make deliberate choices, you make conscious decisions, you have control. Being a resister means that, under a given set of circumstances, you decide to do what you believe is in your best interest and determine not to have that power and control taken away from you." These were revolutionary words twelves years ago. Exploding the Myth of Self-Defense takes you further into heretofore uncharted territory.

Exploding the Myth...takes you on a journey of enlightenment—from facing the omnipresent fear of rape, to conquering this fear and making changes which place you in control of your life.

The concept that rape is an outward manifestation of an inward fear may raise eyebrows of individuals who are sensitive to the issue of blaming the victim. Yet, if you delve deeply into this concept, you will realize that assault is a two way street. Criminals are to blame and are responsible for their crimes. Yet, the criminal will attack the weakest and most vulnerable victim he can find. Our job is to prevent assault and to do this in a way that preserves our dignity and integrity as human beings.

If we want to be in charge of our lives, then we need to take control. With knowledge of their options and new-found skills, victims become resisters. When you become a resister, body language, awareness, and everything about your total being changes. Then personal power becomes an outward manifestation of your inward strength.

ACKNOWLEDGMENTS

I would like to express my thanks to my students who provided me with the feedback and many success stories over the years that have kept me motivated to continue this important work of helping women take control of their lives. I would also like to thank Lene Johnson who had the foresight to bring Self-Defense for Women into the Physical Educational curriculum of San Francisco City College in 1975.

Special thanks go to Nancy Worthington for her creative insights and wonderful cover art. And finally, I especially wish to thank my editor, Jean Gilliam, for her expertise in English grammar and contributions to the writing of this book.

ONE

EXPLODING THE MYTH OF SELF-DEFENSE

An Overview

EXPLODING THE MYTH OF SELF-DEFENSE
An Overview

Introduction

The fear of rape hangs over women's heads during their entire lifetimes. It is a fear which is instilled into them in early childhood. It is a fear which keeps women from achieving their full potential, from being their own persons, from becoming independent—both economically and emotionally. It is a fear that is continuously reinforced by the society in general. It is a fear that is passed on from generation to generation, so that mothers pass it on to their daughters who pass this fear on to their own daughters—all for good reason. The female of our species is subjected to being raped. The incidence of incest, child abuse, sexual harassment, battery, and rape has reached epidemic proportions in our society. A study released in 1992 by the National Victim Center of Arlington, Virginia, and the Crime Victims Research and Treatment Center of Charleston, South Carolina, estimated the incidence of forcible rapes in 1990 to be 683,000 —more than five times larger than the National Crime Survey figure of 130,000 attempted and completed rapes in the same year.[1]

Money is being poured into the economy for the purpose of categorization, research on victims, and aid for victims. The National Victims Resource Center (NVRC) is a national clearinghouse for victims' information funded by the Office for Victims of Crime, U.S. Department of Justice. It offers a toll-free number to be of assistance in providing: national victimization statistics; federally sponsored victim-related research studies; more than 7,000 victim-related books and articles; contacts, addresses, telephone numbers, and information on state victims' compensation programs funded by the Office for Victims of Crime.[2]

What is sorely lacking is support for the prevention of violent crime, i.e., educating our citizens in how to take care of themselves. The National Institutes for Mental Health (NIMH) funded rape prevention studies through the National Center for the Prevention and Control of Rape. The NIMH reorganized in the mid- 1980's and currently provides minimal funding for research into rape prevention.

Women, however, have come a long way in the past twenty years. They have achieved degrees of financial independence, of career choices, and of professional advancement unheard of before. Still, a tremendous duality exists. A women who is dynamite in the board room, when threatened with assault on the streets, many times falls apart. On the job, she is intelligent, bright, assertive, and self-determined. Yet, on the streets, the moment she is threatened with attack, she panics, freezes, and is victimized.

Blaming the Victim

A victim is not to be blamed! Society is very good at pointing the finger of blame at the victim. In fact, blaming the victim is a form of social control which, on the one hand, exonerates the rapist and, on the other hand, further punishes the woman who has been raped. It sends a message loud and clear to both parties, telling the rapist that it is O.K. to rape and telling the rape victim that she did something to cause the rape.

A distinction must be made between blaming the victim for being raped and stating that it is within our power not to be a victim. If you place power and control in the hands of external factors (situational factors, such as time of day or location, or societal factors, such as male violent behavior or a poor economy) then power and control is taken away from the individual who then becomes powerless.

I do not blame the victim. A victim sees no other options. Victim mentality buys into the socialization of powerlessness—a victim has internalized her own oppression. I do not condone the politics of victimization or the perpetuation of victimization. Excluding truly helpless individuals who need to be protected, condoning and supporting victimization is tantamount to condoning powerlessness. Give support and counseling to the survivor of an assault. Then teach her how to regain her power and control over her life so that she never is a victim again!

The Myth of Self-Defense

The myth of self-defense is that the enemy on which we are focusing our defense is outside of ourselves—whether he be a rapist, mugger, or other criminal. When you focus your efforts on someone or something out of your control, then you are not in charge of the situation.

The reality of self-defense is that the enemy we are battling is within ourselves. Instead of directing our attention into rehabilitating rapists or getting men to change, we must pinpoint our focus on ourselves. When we change our focus, when we conquer the enemy within, we become powerful. We have control.

Women Face A Common Enemy

Women face a common enemy. In order to become a totally whole, integrated self, each woman must battle this enemy. Although participants in women's victimization, man and society at large are not her main enemy. Nighttime is not the enemy. To find this enemy, she must look within herself because the enemy is within. The enemy is a duality. It must be named and it must be conquered. The enemy is her own fear and her own socialization.

Rape is an outward manifestation of an inward fear! Fear can be described as a box which has very distinct limits. If you are trapped within this box you are a prisoner. Your very life, your own freedom, and your very movements are controlled. Once you conquer this fear and lift the lid off this box, a great weight is also lifted and you feel free. Once again (or for the first time) you feel in control of your life. Night is beautiful and is not your enemy. You can enjoy taking a walk or hiking in the woods. You will have the freedom to go where you choose and to do what you wish to do without having the heavy weight of fear hang over your head.

The Fear of Fighting

So why does fear control women's lives? Much of this has to do with the fear of fighting. When threatened with attack or when attacked, many women are afraid to fight back. In my self-defense classes, one of the first topics my students discuss is the fear of fighting. The reasoning behind this discussion is that, if these fears are brought out into the open, the self-defense/rape myths can be debunked and then can be dealt with. Common fears include:

- The fear of getting injured
- The fear of hurting anyone
- The fear of the assailant's being larger or stronger
- The fear of male power and violence in general
- The fear of freezing or panicking
- The fear of being ineffective
- The fear of the assailant's having a weapon
- The fear of angering the assailant
- The fear of getting too angry and loosing control

These fears will be debunked and dealt with in Chapter 2—The Psychology of Empowerment.

Self-Defense Training as Survival Training

How do you overcome these fears? Self-defense training must be thought of as survival training. It is survival training in the same bent as CPR , lifesaving training, or fire-drill training. What this means is that all of these forms of training teach you how to respond appropriately in a crisis situation. You learn what works and what doesn't work. Through knowledge and training, you are able to control the situation and make choices, rather than having the situation control you.

Survival training in self-defense incorporates learning certain principles and skills, such as learning the anatomy of an assault or learning the definition of what constitutes sexual harassment. Survival training incorporates learning how to replace fear with anger when threatened with attack. It teaches you how to act, rather than freeze, in a crisis. Physical skills must also be learned to back up the psychological ones. Although fairly simple to learn, they must be practiced so that they become second nature to you, so that, if you choose to employ them, they become automatic. Having the knowledge and ability to take care of yourself permits you the power of choice.

The Point of Power

The basis from which all personal power and freedom arise is the sense of self, i.e., self-esteem. Self-defense begins with the sense of self. The point of power is within each of us. Our own power, our personal power, is our power and control over our lives. If we blame external forces for our problems and for our lack of control, then these forces control us. When we tap into our own sense of power we, and not the assailant, make the decisions. The only decision that we allow the assailant to make is how fast and how far he can run (if he still is able to run away).

TWO

THE PSYCHOLOGY OF EMPOWERMENT

THE PSYCHOLOGY OF EMPOWERMENT

Bridging The Gap

Over the past twenty years, women have made major inroads into heretofore sparsely traveled territory. We have become financially independent; we run successful businesses; we are in management positions in corporations and governmental agencies. We have chosen, and succeed in, careers which have previously been male preserves. Yet, a schism exists which prevents women from becoming totally whole, integrated human beings. Let us take, for example, a successful career woman. She is self-assured and confident. She projects an aura of professionalism and respect. This same woman is walking to her car after work and is come upon by a potential rapist who threatens to kill her if she does not cooperate. This woman falls apart! Why? Moreover, how can she fully respect herself and have full confidence in her abilities when she cannot even take care of herself?

Awareness Is The First Step Toward Change

Nancy Worthington, whose artwork "Cinderella Liberty" is on the front cover of this book, creates sculptures and drawings which reflect conditions in our society. Her statement of art reveals the purpose behind her work: "The images become a catalyst to awaken consciousness... It is my sense of hope for the future that makes me want to facilitate change through awareness for a better, more humane world. I see my art as reaching out to be a connecting point for awareness." [3]

Awareness then is the first step toward change. In order to understand the psychology of empowerment, it is necessary to understand the nature of women's socialization into powerlessness. Only when this consciousness has been awakened can change begin.

The Tennis Court Incident

Recently I was playing a game of doubles at a college in San Francisco. It was 12:00 Noon. The courts were free until 12:10 P.M. at which time members of the tennis team were scheduled to practice. We planned relinquishing the courts at 12:10 P.M. Two young men walked onto our court and demanded that we get off so that they could play. Their body language was pure, raw aggression, and they expected to be obeyed. The other three women that were playing with me immediately fled the court stating that it was O.K. with them and that they would use another court.

I refused to leave and confronted the young men. I hadn't understood their behavior at first because three other courts were free. The spokesperson of the two said that he wanted this specific court because it was the "Number 1" court. I stated that we were playing on this court and that they could have played on any one of the free courts. He said that this would have been the rational thing to do. He wasn't being rational—he just wanted this court and thought that it was his right to be there and that the women should defer to him.

Why did the three women flee from the court? What does this have to do with the socialization of women to be victims? Why did the men feel that it was their prerogative to take over, without consideration for the rights or feelings of these women?

The women left the court because the sum total of their socialization as it existed at that point in their lives left them with no alternatives. They didn't even stop to think. They just reacted!

Victim Behavior Is Learned Behavior

Susan Faludi, in her eye-opening exposé Backlash, discusses a "culture machine" made of codes and cajolings, whispers, threats, and myths which "...move overwhelmingly in one direction: they try to push women back into their 'acceptable' roles... ." [4]

From earliest childhood, females learn that it is a "man's" world—that their place in life is to be subservient to men. In practically every aspect of their lives, they learn that boys or men are more important and that their role is to serve them or be secondary to them.

Males and females are polarized from birth. For a family, the birth of a son is a great event. Boys are taught to be strong and independent. They play together learning how to be strong and independent and how to be cooperative team members as well. They test their strength on each other, and fighting is not uncommon. Boys learn that they will not break in two if they are struck. They learn that, as males, they are important and that they are the conquerors. Neely Tucker of the Knight-Ridder newspapers reported on a 1987 survey in Rhode Island schools which found that one in four middle-school boys thought it was O.K. to force a girl to have sex if he had spent more than $10 on her. Tucker notes that "Reports of aggressive sexual behavior by young boys have been chilling." The author goes on to state that nationwide studies show that one in three women was the victim of sexual assault during her childhood. [5]

Boys' toys encourage adventure and violence. Their role models are active, strong, aggressive heroes. Girls' toys emphasize the passive role of mother and homemaker. Girls nurture. A girl's toy career choice is a nurse as compared to a boy's doctor.

Girls and boys see a world run and dominated by males. They go to the movies and see violent, unemotional males—and these violent males "get their man;" in many scenarios, they rescue "helpless females." In other movies, these male heroes violently "get their women," and these women seem to enjoy being conquered. If a woman plays a strong role in the movies, she is portrayed as evil and is usually destroyed. They watch television and see a repeat of violent males and passive females. The infrequently portrayed aggressive woman still must be rescued by a male hero. The music that they listen to and the magazines and books that they read all perpetuate the glorification of the male and the dehumanization, objectification and secondary role of the female. They see their society being run by males—from the President of the United States to the Supreme Court and to the United State Senate: all branches of government overwhelmingly dominated by men.

In the Fall of 1991 this point was driven home to women—loud and clear. On national television, the Clarence Thomas Supreme Court nomination hearings were broadcast live. Sexual harassment charges were made against Mr. Thomas by Anita Hill. Women viewers were appalled at the way Ms. Hill was humiliated and discredited by an all-male committee which represented a 98% male Senate. A couple of months later, the media continued to demonstrate the powerlessness of females. Live and in color, national television presented the William Kennedy Smith rape trial. Mr. Smith was acquitted, and men were sent a message that they could get away with rape. In both cases, the word of the male was worth more than the word of the female. The men—being in power, being more important, and, therefore being more credible—were believed.

A major problem inherent within this patriarchy is the psychological effect that it has on women. Patriarchy is the cause of low self-esteem in women. With low self-esteem comes powerlessness.

Conquering The Enemy From Within

Now that we have an awareness of the basis of the socialization toward victimization, we can change this base and become powerful. If victim behavior is learned behavior, then it is equally important to realize that resister behavior is also learned behavior.

Women are not born victims. Awareness is the first step toward change. The second step is to consciously change from passive victim behavior to behavior patterns which are active and powerful. In order to become powerful, we must conquer the enemy from within. This enemy is our own fear and our socialization by the society to be victims.

The very essence of self-defense is personal power. Personal power is being in control of your life. It means that you make choices, that you make decisions, that you do what you believe is best for you. And it means that you are determined not to have that power and control taken away from you—which is the very essence of rape. One of the best benefits of developing personal power for self-defense is that, with knowledge, it carries over to the rest of your life. Therefore, once this connection is made, your life changes.

Self-Defense Begins With Self-Esteem

Self-defense begins with self-esteem, i.e., the belief in oneself. You must believe that you are worth fighting for. Notice this duality:

Question: "What would you do if someone threatened you with attack?"
Answer: "I'd be afraid."
Question: "What would you do if someone threatened to harm your child?"
Answer: "I'd kill him."

Just as in nature, where a lioness protects her cub, it is appropriate for a woman to protect her child. The same woman who would be afraid to fight back—who wouldn't have any clue as to how to fight back—would fly into a rage and attack anyone who tried to harm her child. It is socially acceptable to protect one's young. Why would it not be appropriate to protect oneself? It is appropriate for every woman to protect herself. With high self-esteem and self-defense knowledge, she will want to and will be able to.

In order to develop personal power, you must learn to believe in your own sanctity as a human being. You are a unique, worthwhile person. You respect yourself, and thus others respect you. You have the right to live your life the way you choose. No one has any right to try to take your integrity away from you. No one has the right to touch you without your consent. No one has the right to hurt you.

The motive for rape is power. A rapist will try to take your power away by violating your integrity. Left within is a void which becomes filled with fear, depression, and guilt.

New Conditioning

The Russian physiologist Ivan Pavlov demonstrated the process of classical conditioning.[6] In a demonstration of an unconditioned or unlearned response, a dog would salivate in response to food in its mouth. Pavlov then demonstrated a new response—a learned response. He flashed a light shortly before putting food in the dog's mouth. After a time, the dog salivated in response to the flashing light alone. This is called a conditioned response.

When threatened with rape, many women become paralyzed with fear. This paralysis is a conditioned response! It is the result of years and years of socialization into victimization. It is time to learn a new conditioned response: *anger!* In most cases, the appropriate response to a threat is rage. The woman who is a resister immediately responds by getting angry, yelling, and thus unleashing her fury.

It is useful to visualize someone who embodies these resister characteristics. A wonderful fictional person is Towanda

The Avenger. She is found in Fannie Flagg's novel Fried Green Tomatoes At The Whistle Stop Cafe. Towanda The Avenger is the righter of wrongs. Towanda could do anything she liked. "Few people who saw this...pleasant-looking...housewife...could guess that, in her imagination, she was machine-gunning the genitals of rapers and stomping abusive husbands to death in her specially designed. . .boots."[7]

Responding to the Fears of Fighting

Let us now bring out into the open and debunk fears, listed in Chapter 1, which may keep a woman from becoming powerful and fighting back successfully.

The Fear of Getting Injured

This fear arises out of lack of experience in competitive physical activities (such as contact team sports). Boys learn from childhood that if they make physical contact they will not fall apart. In fact, if you have ever played in a competitive sport, you do not even usually feel it if you get punched or shoved or hit with a ball. You only become aware of it the next day when you notice a black and blue mark and wonder where it came from.

The Fear of Hurting Anyone

Female conditioning is to nurture, to heal, and to comfort. It is not to hurt anyone. Each of us must live with our own code of ethics. I personally believe in living my life the way I choose to live it, as long as I am not intentionally hurting anyone else. And I also believe in allowing others to live their lives in the same genre. I do not consider it right to hurt anyone. People need to respect the rights of others. However, when someone tries to violate your rights as a human being or when someone tries to take away your integrity, then all rules are off! It is your right to do whatever you need to do to take care of yourself. If it comes down to hurting an assailant, then you hurt him. In fact, you do more than just hurt him, you incapacitate him. You do this so that he cannot hurt you.

The Fear of the Assailant's Being Larger or Stronger

(See Chapter 9—Physical Self-Defense.)

Relative size or the physical strength of the assailant has little to do with your physical ability to fight back. The limiting factor is really psychological. The assailant would not be attacking you if he expected you to fight back successfully. Your defense is to take him off guard, as you instantly incapacitate him by attacking his vulnerable areas. These areas cannot be protected or strengthened by the assailant. Your target areas are the assailant's weak areas. If the assailant is especially large, you have a bigger advantage. His target areas are larger and, therefore, easier for you to hit, kick, or strike.

The Fear of Male Power and Violence in General

This is socialized conditioning which is broken by a belief in yourself. No one has any right to hurt you. How dare he even try! What gives him the right? The reason he is targeting you is because you are a woman—a "subspecies" to him. He believes he can get away with it. Get furious! A woman's anger terrifies men, and many men panic in the face of a woman's rage. [8]

The Fear of Freezing or Panicking

Many women share this most common of all fears. It is such a universal fear that many of us have nightmares of being attacked and yelling soundlessly. You will not panic in a crisis situation if you are prepared and if you know your options: what has the greatest chance of working, what doesn't work, and what is the appropriate response. Knowledge and practice and the belief in your ability to take care of yourself mark the difference between a potential victim and a resister.

The Fear of Being Ineffective

Self-confidence and the belief in your ability to take care of yourself go a long way in allaying this fear. Knowledge, training, and practicing psychological and physical skills are your best guarantee of effective resistance.

The Fear of The Assailant's Having a Weapon

Most rapists do not carry weapons. In 1989 firearms were used to commit 6% of all reported rapes.[9] You must also realize that most assaults can be prevented through awareness. If threatened by an assailant that displays a lethal weapon, you must choose your appropriate response under the circumstances. Options will be discussed in detail in Chapter 9.

The Fear of Angering the Assailant

In reality, a potential assailant needs to be afraid of angering you! It really doesn't matter how angry an assailant gets. When you physically incapacitate him, he cannot hurt you.

The Fear of Getting Too Angry and Loosing Control

If you are trained in the art of physical and psychological self-defense, you will be in control of the situation. You will know exactly what is occurring . You will, therefore, be able to choose and act on your options so that you have a successful defense.

The Anatomy of an Assault

The next step is to understand the anatomy of an assault. Assailants follow predictable patterns. If you understand these patterns, you can break them.[10]

Targeting

Assailants target their potential victims. They want to be

successful, so they select vulnerable individuals whom they do not expect to be able to fight back. They base their selection on three criteria: who, where, and psychological state.

Who?

An attacker will pick people on the basis of who they are. Individuals who fit into this category include: women; children; disabled people; senior citizens; and people who seem out of place, such as tourists. Individuals in certain professions may be more at risk, such as nurses, real estate agents, or shift workers.

Where?

Location is important. Assailants do not want to be seen or caught; therefore, they look for isolated areas. Assailants like to attack at night or early morning because they have the cover of darkness and fewer people are usually out and about. Isolated areas can be tricky. An isolated area can be your own home if a hostile individual is inside. Your car can be an isolated area. An isolated area can be anyplace where you can be alone with a potential attacker.

Psychological State.

Individuals who are psychologically prepared to fight back are not targeted for attack. Certain categories of people are absolutely unprepared to defend themselves—such as those who are under the influence of drugs or alcohol. The person most frequently chosen by the assailant is someone who is not paying attention. When you drive your car, you pay attention. You have to. Yet, you are still able to listen to music or carry on a conversation. When people park their cars, they turn off the ignition. Many times, along with the ignition, they turn off that part of their consciousness which pays attention—their radar. Then they walk down the street lost in space. Practically every single individual who has reported to me that he or she has been attacked on the street over the past eighteen years has been caught off guard. When asked "Where did the assailant come from?" each person replied "from nowhere."

Testing

After selecting a suitable victim, the assailant then approaches and goes through a testing process. The goal of this testing is to see whether or not the individual can be intimidated. Testing could take many forms such as: casual conversation; threats; harassment; invasion of personal space; physical touching, grabbing, or battery. Potential assailants have been known to cause a distraction, such as a minor car accident, or to work in pairs.

A friend and I went to see a matinee performance of a play at a theatre in San Francisco. The theatre was located in a very seedy neighborhood. After the performance, we started to drive out of the area when a very dirty suspicious-looking man ran up to the car and threw a wine bottle under the front tire. I had no choice but to run over it. We both winced at the crunching sound. As I was driving over the wine bottle, a very nicely dressed woman ran over to the car and yelled, "Your tire is going flat!" I said to my friend, "I would rather drive home on the rims of these tires than stop in this neighborhood." A few blocks later we stopped, got out, and checked the tires. There was no flat. The two were a criminal pair, and they were trying to trick me into stopping the car for robbery or assault.

Attack

If you fail the intimidation test the assailant will attack.

Breaking The Pattern

How to Prevent Targeting

You may be in a target group by virtue of who you are. You cannot change who you are. You may be in a target group because of your location. Many times you cannot or do not choose to change your location. So what can you change? *Your attitude!* If you follow one simple step, you will considerably reduce your risk of being targeted. *Pay attention!*

When you walk down the street, you need to be aware. You body language indicates that you are alert; that you know where you are going and what you are doing; that you respect yourself. You walk with confidence and self-assurance.

If you notice someone attempting to target you, (or if you consider the situation dangerous,) you magnify your level of awareness. You then send out "Don't mess with me!" signals. "Don't mess with me!" clearly indicates that you are alert, that you are aware, and that nobody had better approach you.

Countering the Testing Phase

If you are approached, you must clearly indicate to the potential assailant that you refuse to be intimidated, no matter what! This means that you must convince the assailant that you mean business. Your body language, your verbal language, and your eye contact all say the same thing: "Don't mess with me!" Then, your combined message rings loud and clear: "If you come near me, you will be sorry that you were ever born."

If You Are Attacked or About To Be Attacked

At this point, you immediately transform. You take all the anger that has ever built up inside of you in your entire lifetime and blast it at the assailant. You reach down into your very innermost being and yell a furious battle cry. You create a very strong, impenetrable force field. If necessary, you physically incapacitate the assailant, then run. Every single success story that has ever been reported to me contains these same ingredients. The resister immediately got angry; yelled viciously; attacked, if necessary; and ran away.

Time: 10:30 P.M.
Location: A dangerous neighborhood
Condition of streets: dark and deserted

My partner and I were driving back to our office after an evening seminar when the engine of our car overheated. I maneuvered the stalled car into a bus stop. The bus stop was located in front of a seedy bar. The street was deserted except for two "sleazy characters" who were standing in front of the bar. We got out of the car. My partner stood watch as I poured water into the radiator. She momentarily turned toward me to see how things were going. Out of "nowhere" a man appeared. He towered over my partner (who is tall herself), came up very close to her, and menaced her with a pipe wrench.

This was a classic assault pattern. The assailant had targeted us as: two women, broken down car, middle of the night, isolated area, not paying attention. He then tested his potential victim by invading her personal space and by threatening her with a weapon. If she could be intimidated, he would attack.

She immediately went at this man with anger and outrage. She yelled viciously and threatened him with her fists. My partner turned into "Towanda The Avenger" [11] and created such a force field of fury that he dropped the wrench and tripped on the curb as he was trying to run away. The two "sleazy characters" that were standing in front of the bar ran inside. "Towanda" had cleared the streets!

THREE

STORIES OF EMPOWERMENT AND SUCCESS

"If She Can Do It, So Can I!"

STORIES OF EMPOWERMENT AND SUCCESS
"If She Can Do It, So Can I!"

Ever since I began teaching self-defense in 1974, I have received in turn something special from participants in my classes. It is this special bonus that has kept me motivated all these years and that has encouraged me to work even harder to help women take control of their lives. Stories of success and empowerment must be told and must be shared with other people. I have selected some of the best stories and experiences to share with you. The media are filled with accounts of women and children being raped and beaten. These scare stories tend to push women into a box of fear which paralyzes them.

Success stories are inspirational, set an example, and give us the courage and strength to change. As you read them, note the common threads running through each story. Each woman has conquered her innermost fears, and by this trial by fire each has forged her way to new inward strength.

Diane

Diane is a 98 pound, 4'11", black woman who is the most formidable person I know. She projects an aura of self-respect and self-confidence. She easily traverses even the worst areas of the city. I asked Diane to tell us where this inner strength came from and to share the secrets of her "street smarts."

"My mother came from poverty to provide for her family and a made a success of her life. During all her trials and tribulations she endured and persevered because she wanted a better life. She was so determined and strong that she overcame everything that was against her. Being poor, black and having a family to raise as a single parent, and not having any support except that from God, my mother did the impossible. I am so impressed and proud of my mother it's just beyond words. My mother is my greatest inspiration in my life.

"The strength and support my mother has given me has made me believe in myself. I will not be stopped from doing what I have to do. I am strong because I have a strong role model. I stand for no nonsense from anyone. She has taught me to depend on myself, go after what I want, and never settle for less. A man doesn't make a woman, a woman is.

"Wherever I go in the city, I go with a purpose. I don't fear being accosted by anyone. My pace is often fast. I am alert; I am aware of where I am. I know where I am going. People don't bother me. I speak when spoken to or I'll speak first, but I don't stop and converse with anyone. Even when people try to talk to me I give them a smile and keep going. I've never been disrespected by anyone on the streets. I am constantly looking around and behind me no matter where I am. Sometimes I am so tired that my face says 'don't bother me.' I am the worst person to deal with when I am tired, so 'stay out of my face!' I have that look that also says 'bother me and you're dead meat!' I face people and situations. I watch people and keep going wherever it is I am going. I don't think that I intimidate people. I am just a short, little black women on the move. My back is straight and my stride is that of a confident person. When I walk, even in the worst areas in the city, I stand at the bus stops without worrying about anyone bothering me, and it is the same when I am on the buses. I can sit in the back on the worst bus routes and show no fear. Why walk in fear? But whenever a situation may arise in which I would need to react, I will act with confidence.

"I don't like threats. So far this has not happened to me

either. I don't take them kindly. No one has the right to try to take my confidence in myself away. I won't allow that. I have too many things to do and places to go. Why let someone take myself away from myself? I am important to me. I simply will not allow my space and peace of mind to be violated."

Reyna

"One of the reasons that I took the self-defense class was because the bus was my only means of transportation. It seemed that every time I was at the bus stop or on the bus I was getting harassed—people (especially men) were saying very rude things to me and invading my space both physically and emotionally. I would tell them to leave me alone but they wouldn't. I felt angry and victimized. This was a time in my life when I was getting in touch with my body in a new way. So when I started taking the class, I learned the power of my body. For example, I learned that 40 pounds of pressure would break a kneecap. I knew that I could kick and run, and this was very liberating and empowering. I took the class for two semesters. After about four or five weeks into the first semester I noticed that nobody was bothering me anymore. I was standing at the bus stop and was ready to use the self-defense techniques —but I was projecting my energy differently and was more grounded. I felt connected to the ground, and wasn't isolated anymore. I was now empowered and in control. In the 17 years since I took this class, I have never gotten hassled again."

Mary

"I was walking home from school. It was around one or maybe even two in the afternoon. I was minding my own business, and two guys started wooing and whistling. I ignored them. After a while I noticed that one of the guys started following me closely and said something indecent. I turned around right away and yelled at him, calling him every name I could think of. I can't forget the expression on his face. He was shocked! He stopped right in his tracks and just stood there stunned with my behavior. I walked away feeling really good and in control because I didn't let him harass or intimidate me."

Lisa

"It was 6:00 P.M. and I was on my way from work to the train station. I felt someone was following me. I turned around to see. The man behind me stopped and lit a cigarette. I continued walking. I got that feeling again and turned around again. The same man stopped walking once more. This stopping and starting happened three times.

"Traffic started coming down the street then and the man thought this was his opportunity. He started running up behind me. This really scared me because two years ago that was how I got mugged; a man ran up behind me, knocked me down and dragged me for a block by my leather purse. I ended up in physical therapy for months. Since I was mugged I have been afraid that I wouldn't be able to handle the same sort of situation without getting hurt. Now I have renewed confidence. Not only did I take care of the problem, I prevented it from happening. I turned, got in my stance and put my hand on my tear gas so he could see. He stopped dead in his tracks and after a moment he decided to run through traffic. I didn't even have to use the tear gas. He seemed to know exactly what it was and didn't want anything to do with it."

Barbara

"I was taking my daily three mile walk on a country lane when a young man pulled his truck over in front of me and at tempted to lure me into the bushes under the pretense of helping him catch a big Jack rabbit. He kept coming toward me, trying to get me to stop walking and accompany him on this rabbit chase in the willows. When he got within 20 feet of me, I quickly clipped my tear gas canister off my belt and held it up toward him and gave him my best 'don't mess with me ' look. I continued to walk backwards so I could keep my eye on him and keep my tear gas pointed at him. He immediately changed his direction and disappeared into the bushes.

"I am firmly convinced that my resistant attitude and my holding the tear gas in a threatening *don't try it* manner discouraged him from being more aggressive."

Irene

"I just returned from a four month stay in New York City. I believe that your course and book [Are You A Target?] saved me from being mugged and beaten-up.

" I knew I would be working in a bad area in New York. I made two mistakes. I left my tear gas in the studio, and I did not take into consideration that it was a deserted Sunday in a warehouse district. Although the studio was filled with other artists, once I shut both outer doors behind me, I was alone and trapped. I was leaving the studio to make a quick run to the art store on Canal Street and was accosted in the stairwell. I do believe instinct plays a big part. I did feel that I could not relinquish any power to him by giving him my purse. I was able to summon up my anger—unleash it—and me, a petite 5'3, send a 6' mugger running. One of the things that helped was actually 'practicing' bringing up that anger in front of a mirror when I was alone. I guess I was so afraid I wouldn't be able to that I needed extra reassurance that I could do it.

"A week later, on a Sunday again, one of the women in the program who was taking laundry down the stairs at the

Y.M.C.A. on 34th Street was beaten up by some lunatic in the stairwell. After that we never used the stairs alone. She was so affected that she left the program and returned to Chicago. But I can't help wondering whether she would have been able to escape injury had she had some self-defense awareness and training. In my instance, standing up for myself, not allowing someone to hurt me by getting angry as hell worked. I do not feel powerless anymore."

Joan

"I first came to the city in 1968 and took the usual risks of youth at the time and was lucky. In 1986, I returned from a rural area and was rudely awakened to the change in the streets by: (1) having my purse grabbed while waiting for a bus; (2) being lucky enough to get help from a passing taxi driver in fighting off attackers on a lonely street.

"I had received my tear gas license in 1976 but lost it with my purse in the theft. I was unable to replace it. This situation brought me to Judith [Fein] and her book Are You A Target? which brought in a new world of meaning. Knowing the awareness and being prepared mentally as well as physically keeps me from getting picked as a victim.

"I got my first stun gun and I now enjoy frequent dog walks in off-leash areas, able to defend my animals from aggressors of the four leg variety. (Pit bulls...are easily warded off from the sound of the [stun gun] arc along with a loud 'No!') Tear gas in this case is back-up from the vicious owner attack. When you're ready, nothing happens. Two of my women friends tragically were not."

Laurie

"On Easter Sunday I drove home from Los Angeles with

three friends. We were unpacking the car at the street curb. I was left by myself to watch the car. Two drunk boys, approximately 17 and 19 (street punks/gang members) came up to me—one on each side. They harassed me by saying very obscene things to me. Normally I would just have ignored what they were saying, but it was approximately 2 A.M. on a very deserted street. I felt that I was in danger. I got angry. I looked the leader of the two right in the eyes and yelled at him to leave me alone and ordered them to get away from me. They stopped, looked at me, then crossed the street and left in their car without saying another word to me."

Mary Jo

"In 1986 I received my tear gas training and permit to carry tear gas. This was and is the best investment I ever made. It gave me a sense of security, as I had had many terrifying boyfriend experiences in the past working as a night bartender.

"On this particular night, I had a very nice crowd; no problems, just happy people having fun. When it got it be closing time, people left through the front exit. After locking the door, I went to check the rear exit to make sure it was secured, and checked to make sure that there was no one left in the rest rooms. A man came out of the men's room and astonished me. It was a complete surprise because everyone said that he already left. I had my tear gas in my hands, attached to my keys. This made me feel very secure. He tried to rape me, shoving me against the corner close to the rear exit. He was breathing hard, telling me that he was crazy about me, and that he just couldn't control himself. I know him and his family and didn't just want to shoot him with the tear gas. It finally got to the critical point, so I told him, 'Do you know what this is in my hand? This is tear gas and I'm going to let you have it if you don't leave right now!' With that, he quickly let go of me, backed-up, and his arms went straight up as if I had a gun. 'O.K., O.K., I'm sorry. I'll leave. I just don't know what came over me.' I pushed him out the door.

"I was never so happy in all my life to have my tear gas with me. It saved me without ever having to use it. I have noticed that men, including some employers, have and show a lot of respect for you when they know you carry it. ...I also might add that this same man is respectful of me now, and always waves in a friendly manner."

Jennifer

"I had a small but very empowering 'success story'. Basically I told a man, in no uncertain terms, to stop staring at me and he did."

Carolyn

"I had gone to an afternoon movie and on my way home stopped at the bank. It was about 6:05 P.M., just getting dark, as I walked into the foyer where the automated teller machine is. I had just punched in my identification numbers when I heard a distinct *swishing* sound outside the door. At this point, I paused, turned to see who or what was making the sound and I saw a person walking by in an exercise suit. I thought, 'Don't be paranoid. This is a safe place.' But as I continued the transaction, I reached into my purse and pulled out my tear gas canister. As the teller machine clicked on about its business of giving me $60.00 in cash, I asked myself why I was pulling it out. It was an act without much thought attached. I rarely pull out that canister.

"Cash safely stowed in my purse, I stepped back out to the street and turned the corner into the parking lot where I had left my car. The parking lot is literally a dead end, a high concrete walled canyon. It was then I saw a man *swishing* along the lot toward me. I guess you could say I was cornered. He was mumbling obscenities, 'fuck, Goddamn you...' etc., and the thought that occurred to me was, 'Now what do I do?' The answer was 'Walk confidently and powerfully to your car.' It was then I felt the tear gas canister in my hand and I raised it to waist level just to be ready. He continued to angle toward me as he walked. Now confident that I could handle any potential assault, I *was* able to walk bravely past him without even a quiver. I thought, 'Go right ahead buddy, try something. I don't mind trying out my new canister on you.' I reached my car safely and said a prayer of thanks. Thinking back, I realize it was a set-up, that he saw me in the ATM foyer and he went right to the parking lot where I would be likely to go. If there was any thought in his head of making a quick hit and run, I am sure it was thwarted by my undaunted confidence and keen awareness."

Mary

"I'm out on a gray, overcast day. My 58 year old mom and little poodle are walking along the southernmost end of Ocean Beach. 'Why don't people walk on this part of the beach?' my mother asks me several times. 'I don't know' is my only reply. It is beautiful on this private isolated beach, the only sounds being the rhythmic pounding and roar of ocean waves and the frolicking birds who run up and down the shore with the changing tide. I feel so happy and contented with my seemingly private stretch of ocean; I feel almost powerful in my bond with nature. I am one with her power and her beauty. ...I wish we could stay here forever.

"It is getting dark and we decide to hurry back to the car. On the way, I see a group of young, scruffy-looking people—7 or 8 in number. Their eyes are glazed and they look like sewer rats to me. The hairs prickle up on the back of my neck as one tall guy comes running at us with his arms overhead in an attempt to intimidate me. I feel alarmed but not panicked. My mom and dog are walking next to me. We are all sensing a threat to our well-being. We walk quickly while he follows about ten feet behind taunting us. He picks up a long rope-like object and swings it over his head. I turn to my mother and sternly demand my canister of tear gas [which is in her beach bag]. 'Get it out now!!!' He stops. He hears my words of anger, feels my anger and sees my tear gas canister. He stops following us."

Jackie

"I was walking through City College toward the outskirts of the campus when a mugger suddenly came up from behind, and put his arms around my neck. I felt something cold on my face. He got me to the ground. At that point I saw his knife. He said: 'Don't shout, all I want is your money!' He saw my ring and started to say: 'Oh this ring will bring in a couple of grand.' At this point I got very angry and yelled loudly and furiously at him. He jumped up and ran away. I have never seen anyone run so fast up a hill before!"

Beverly

"I live alone with my overly friendly dog, in a largish house. The other evening I was upstairs standing at my desk. The house was absolutely quiet—no T.V., no music—silent. My dog raised her ears and looked at the stairs—there stood a man looking at me.

"For a moment, I went limp.Then your [Dr. Fein's] voice came through loud and clear in my head—'Get mad, be aggressive.' <u>So</u> ...'Who <u>are</u> you and what are you doing in my house?' He mumbled something about needing directions. I had left one of my canisters on the desk. I grabbed it thinking it might intimidate him, saying '<u>Get out</u>!' Well, he didn't move. Again your voice, 'You have only one—two seconds to act. I sprayed him. The propellant worked. He turned his face away, took off his glasses and again mumbled. I couldn't believe he was still standing there and real anger began to take over. 'Get out of my house' I yelled, and again your voice, 'First the eyes, then the mouth.' So he got another face full before he finally backed down the stairs and stumbled out the front door. I called 911."

Magelena

"It was an Easter Sunday at 11:00 P.M. and I was traveling downtown on my way to work a graveyard shift. My instinct told me that I would encounter trouble. I knew that few people would be traveling downtown on a holiday that late at night—except those up to no good.

"The instant I saw *him*, I knew that he was one of those people. As he entered the train, he went out of his way to bump into some exiting passengers. Of course, few would challenge this man. At 6'3 and 225 lbs, he knew that.

"What immediately bothered me about this man was that he spotted me before he had entered the train. He stared intently at me, his gaze unwavering. I tried to appear as confident as possible but felt myself shrinking beneath his malignant glare. His large yellowed eyes revealed that he was probably on drugs. They contrasted sharply with his dark skin and angular features. Further, he wore dark clothing and a very tall cowboy hat, giving him the appearance of a giant.

"He was obviously a master of intimidation. He sat facing me with his legs spread open, his pelvis thrust outward. An all-knowing grin was fixed on his face. This man was outrageously pompous. Most likely, his career as a rapist had been successful.

"I tried to calm myself in order to gain some control of the situation. I had experienced a truly awful day and I was extremely tired. I was certain that he could sense my vulnerable state.

"At last, the train arrived at my stop. I tried exiting at the last moment, but to no avail. He followed me off the train. Unfortunately, the platform was completely deserted. I walked over to a phone booth. I believed now that I was testing him. I wanted to give him the impression that I was meeting someone upstairs.

"But, he was too self-assured. He waited calmly, never faltering. Finally, I finished my phone call. I walked towards an escalator. He walked with me.

"Suddenly, I decided to take control. First, I began to assess the situation. I felt that he didn't have any advantage over me, with the exception of his size. I, on the other hand, had the advantage of physical skills training as well as a canister of tear gas on me. Most importantly, however, I had the benefit of coherence and enough psychological training to call his bluff.

"I quickly laid out my strategy. I would confront him. If that didn't work, I would spray him with my tear gas. And finally, I would deliver a severe blow to his knee if he persisted. I began to fuel my anger, converting my fear to angry energy. I was tired of being afraid of taking public transportation when I had a right to. I was tired of being targeted because of my gender and my size [98 lbs]. And finally I was tired of this goon harassing me!

"I jabbed my pointer finger at his face and commanded 'You had better not be following me. Not me!' His expression changed, he backed up and walked away."

Victoria

"One evening about 5:30 P.M., as I was walking to a workout, I was passed by a heavyset man. The sidewalk was narrow so I moved further to the curb to accommodate this man. He made a lewd remark to me as he passed. I saw him out of the corner of my eye and ignored him. However, I increased my pace and stride. He then stopped and said something else. By then I was several yards away from him. He turned around and pursued me, saying vulgar things to me. The faster I walked, the faster he walked. It seemed like a long time that we had been walking like this when in fact it was only a few more yards. I could see his clothes out of the corner of my eye, and I saw him reaching for my shoulder. A feeling inside me warned me he was going to hurt me if he got the chance.

"At this point, I jumped forward quickly, got into my stance and turned around. I yelled quite loudly and fiercely, and with all my weight pushed him back with my hands. I then jumped back so that I was out of his reach and then got into a position to slug him with my right fist. His back hit the wall and the fence which ran waist-level up along the wall. He bounced back and looked confused.

"He saw me and I looked very pissed off. He put his hands up to cover his face to protect himself and then took off running back the way he came from originally.

"I think a lot of this was my instinct to protect myself and my feeling of anger at the idea that someone could feel that they had the right to intimidate me with obscene language, touch me and force his will on me. First I was scared, but I think when the situation really was a reality, I became mad and wanted to protect myself."

Eve

"I was grateful to get my first canister of tear gas. It may have saved my life. Two and a half years ago my friend and I were attacked one night. She was being strangled by her own leather throng necklace. I attempted to get him off of her. My four years of karate did no good. The assailant then threw me to the ground. From the ground I was able to get the tear gas out of my back pocket and spray. The attacker yelled 'Gas!' and he, along with a second attacker, fled."114

Kathryn

"I am out on the street at 2:15 A.M. every weekday to catch the bus to work. A couple of weeks ago a young man came up to me at my bus stop and said, 'I need twenty dollars. Don't take out your mace or I'll slash you.' So I took out my knife, and angrily said to him, 'not if I slash you first, bastard!,' and then screamed my guts out. I wound up chasing him down the street, knife in my hand."

Jenny

"I was shopping in a store which mostly carried women's clothing—a few men's items were in the back. A suspicious-looking man came into the store and hung around in the back. I had read in the paper that a number of recent robberies had been committed in small stores in this vicinity. I felt uneasy because of the way the man was acting—he was pretending to look at men's items. I decided to pay for the things that I had already selected and leave. When I went up to the cashier to pay, the man started walking toward the front of the store. He left the store just before I finished paying. I thought he may have stepped aside so that he could grab my purse. I waited until I saw him walk across the front of the store. Then, with a purposeful stride—my purse held tightly in front of me, keys ready in hand—I walked out so that I would be behind him. He walked very slowly ahead of me. I stepped off the curb and walked to a row of cars ahead, where my car was parked. He stepped off the curb and started coming toward me (he was 10 feet away). I looked him straight in the eye with a 'school ness, my confident walk, and my actions which sent out 'Don't mess with me!' signals. He turned, stepped back on the sidewalk, and walked away from me without looking back. I was 69 years old at the time."

Bonnie

"I have always been a free spirit and have traveled extensively by myself. A few years ago though, I noticed feeling reluctant to venture out on my own. All those years of all those people expressing their worry and concern over my independent adventures finally took their toll! Around this time I learned of your classes. Two thing happened. First, I took a quantum leap in opening up to the realization of the real dangers in our own world and accepting them as fact. Second, I gave myself the precious gift of my freedom and independence.

"Now I am realistic about the danger of the 'real world' and I am a free person. Thank you for what you are doing for women."

Marie

"I have been married for a number of years and am a mother of two boys. I grew up in a conservative and traditional family and had learned, more from viewing role models than any direct instructions, that women should always be submissive and are the weaker gender—not only physically weaker, but mentally and psychologically too. For years I submitted to my husband's wishes and always went along with all his decisions. I couldn't go anywhere without him, I couldn't go out with friends on my own, not even to the store without him driving me. I was afraid to make a commitment to any function because it always caused embarrassment when he decided he didn't want to go. It got to the point where I isolated myself from friends and shunned meeting people.

"Taking this [self-defense for women] class has opened my eyes to the fact that I have choices and can make decisions on my own, as my own person. It helped me develop the confidence to make those decisions and act on them, without the pressure and fear of failure or being frowned upon for straying from my accepted role. It has helped me overcome the fear of being a woman in a man's world.

"By the middle of the semester I was going out with my girlfriends again and having fun. I even gained enough courage to walk into a function with a girlfriend and start conversations with people we met there. If I had done the same things some months before I would have hidden myself in a corner, trying to be as inconspicuous as possible. I would have cowered in fear because I didn't have the self-confidence or self-esteem to deal with that type of situation.

"Learning about power and anger and taking action has helped me gain the strength and courage to set my goals and make plans to achieve them. These last few months have definitely been the most fulfilling time of my adult life. I have grown and become a whole person. And definitely a happier one."

Christina

"In childhood, I was victimized by abuse, a dysfunctional family, and a sexist society. I struggled through alcoholism, manic-depression, breast cancer, and immune system conditions since receiving chemotherapy. When I was in early recovery, I was raped. I know from experience that this violent assault was not about sex, but about power—and it traumatically pointed out to me the profound depths of my powerlessness.

"I have employed many therapies in my process of healing. The psychological attitudes combined with the physical skills of 'self-defense' have greatly helped in overcoming my feeling of victimization by transforming my hurt, fear, guilt, and shame into acceptance, confidence, courage and the dignity of myself and my body. I found an appropriate channel for the expression of anger in the practice of response to an attack. I learned how to be strong and still keep my positive sensitivity by protecting it. Further, this experience has helped me be and feel centered in my body. It is an important part of my ongoing process of development and empowerment to transform fear into faith. Due to my financial disability, I live in a dangerous neighborhood. Though my new awareness will decrease the probability of an attack, I can actually visualize myself fighting back if necessary. I am not afraid."

Eve

"Learning the psychological and self-defense techniques has proven invaluable in my life and my development as a contributing member of society. These skills and strengths have assisted me in all areas of my life, including improved effectiveness in my professional work, as well as increased effectiveness in communicating with colleagues, family, friends and strangers. I have also gained increased energy to tackle the difficulties in my life because I have been freed of the weight of fear of attack and physical injury.

"The knowledge and self-defense techniques that I learned are crucial to all women, from young children to the elderly, including those of us who are able-bodied and those that struggle with physical handicaps. It is amazing to have experienced the acquisition of unfathomable power, both psychologically and physically. The [self-defense] class helps people transform from frightened citizens or victims of violence and/or abuse into whole, strong, blossoming individuals. This transformation is one of the strongest, most empowering experiences I have had in my life."

Harriet

"One early morning at my tennis club I was using the ball machine. It was warm. Four of our indoor courts open into the street, and I opened the two doors at my court. Normally when I do that I move my gear, including my purse, to the far side of the court so if someone has any ideas they would literally have to cross the court to take anything. However, this morning I was lax and did not do that. As I was hitting balls I noticed a well-dressed man in his late 20's standing in the doorway looking around. I looked at him, the tennis pro on the next court noticed him also and looked at him. The young man stayed there for a few moments and then disappeared. About fifteen minutes later I noticed something out of the corner of my eye. Somehow I immediately knew that it was that young man, and that he had taken my wallet. I grabbed my racket and broke the four minute mile record for my age (or any other) running after him. He was just sauntering up the street thinking, I'm sure, that he really put one over on that lady. As I was dashing up the street I thought that he could easily have a knife or gun, but he didn't know I was coming because the traffic noise muffled the noise of my sneakers on the pavement, and my weapon was the element of surprise. I got so close to him that I could have put my arms around him, and whacked him with all of my might with my racket on the side of his head. I yelled, 'Give me back my wallet!' He turned around, stunned, and my wallet dropped out of his jacket to the sidewalk in front of both of us. I proceeded to bend over, picked up my wallet and then beat the hell out of him yelling, 'How dare you take my wallet—what do you think you are doing?' And he said, 'Lady, Lady,' while trying to shield himself from my blows. In the meantime, the tennis pro on the court next to mine looked over and saw that I was gone and she and her student dashed out the door and saw me beating this 180 lb. guy who looked as if he pumped iron. They ran up the street. As soon as the young man saw them, he turned around and ran. It will be a long time before he picks on a grey-haired lady in tennis shoes!"

FOUR

RAPE AVOIDANCE AND DEFENSE STRATEGIES
What Research Tells Us

RAPE AVOIDANCE AND DEFENSE STRATEGIES
What Research Tells Us

Conflicting Advice

Women have been given conflicting advice as to what to do when confronted with the threat of assault. This advice ranges all the way from "immediately and forcefully resist" to "be passive and cooperate with the rapist." I have heard good advice but also outrageous advice, such as to try to hide under a car so that the rapist would not be able to reach you! Other common erroneous recommendations include: reason with them, tell them you have a horrible disease, kick them in the groin, scream, and even put your finger down your throat and vomit. None of these common recommendations is effective. Another form of advice is no advice. For example, a crime prevention officer might say, "You can't prepare ahead of time for these things. I wouldn't want to give you advice which may get your hurt." (Yet, this same police officer has gone through the police academy and spends many hours on the range practicing his skill with a handgun.)

Why have women been given conflicting advice? Part of this advice is given by law enforcement authorities whose area of expertise is in areas other than rape resistance and self-defense. The police deal mainly with victims. A rape survivor, brought into the hospital by law enforcement officers, is traumatized. The police, many times, have no contact with people who successfully resist assault, since the incident is frequently not reported.

A second reason for poor advice is social control. Rape avoidance myths abound. Women generally are given traditional advice, such as:

> (1) If you fight back, such action will only excite the assailant and most probably will result in serious injury to you.
> (2) If you are threatened with assault, try to change the rapist's mind using guile: e.g., tell him that you have V.D., or that you are menstruating, or that you have some horrible illness; or pretend that you are insane.
> (3) If you can, humanize the situation so that the assailant will see you as a human being.

These types of recommendations keep women dependent and restrict their lives. They do not stop rape.[12]

Another explanation is deeply rooted in the human psyche and can be traced back thousands and thousands of years: socialization and sex-role stereotyping. Women are seen as weak, passive, and unable to take care of themselves. Therefore, they must have protectors; they need men to protect them from other men. It is unthinkable for a woman to cross the line and fight physically. Susan Brownmiller in her excellent book, Against Our Will, painstakingly details the psychological, sociological, and historical basis of rape in our society.[13]

Early Self-Defense Classes

When I first started teaching self-defense for women in 1974, I had very little information to go on other than my background in Tae kwon do (Korean karate.) Teaching fighting techniques didn't seem to me to be enough. Then I found a wonderful book, Against Rape, by Andra Media and Kathleen Thompson,[14] which opened my eyes. I could not put this book down! I realized that self-defense for women was much more than physical skills. It was really self-defense against rape. The more I read the book, the angrier I became. For me, the psychology of rape resistance was born in this book. From then on, I taught women both physical defense skills and psychological skills. Success stories started to come in. Then, in 1975, I read an article by Dr. James Selkin in Psychology Today.[15] Dr. Selkin had studied victim and resister reactions in assaultive rape. Dr. Selkin offered a behavioral analysis which depicted the difference between victim and resister behavior. To my delight, Dr. Selkin's advice on physical resistance mirrored my own, which is—in most cases—to immediately and forcefully resist.

Research into Rape Avoidance and Resistance

Studying rape resistance research can be helpful to us in determining how to prepare ourselves ahead of time to respond appropriately in a crisis situation. We can search for the answers to such questions as:

- What strategies are effective?
- What strategies are ineffective or even harmful?
- What is the difference in effectiveness of strategies if the victim and assailant know each other?
- What strategies are effective if the assailant has a weapon?
- Do women suffer injury if they physically resist?

Selkin studied 32 women who were raped and 23 women who avoided rape.[16] He found clear-cut differences in the way rape resisters and rape victims felt and behaved during the assault. "...rape resisters are more likely to experience rage and anger when confronted by an assailant. Resisters are more likely to experience an emotional state conducive of action and vigorous outcry. Victims, on the other hand, experience emotions which can be described as akin to physical and mental paralysis. The extensive use of adjectives such as shocked, frozen, panicked, and terrified to describe their feelings during the assault suggests immobility and acquiescence as their most likely mode of response to the rape threat."[17]

Pauline Bart's book, Stopping Rape,[18] is based on research funded by the now disbanded Center for the Prevention and Control of Rape at the National Institute of Mental Health. The study was based on an analysis of 94 interviews of women. Of these, in the two years prior to the interview, 51 had been attacked and avoided rape, and 43 had been raped.

Bart examined five active resistance strategies: (1) fleeing or trying to flee; (2) physical resistance or force; (3) screaming or yelling; (4) cognitive verbal techniques—including reasoning with the attacker, trying to con him, insisting that she wasn't interested, flattering and/or attempting to make him see her as a human being; and (5) pleading. The effect of environmental intervention (such as a police car or passerby happening along) and the presence of no strategies were also analyzed.[19]

Active Resistance Strategies

Fleeing or Trying to Flee:
Of the 21 women who fled or tried to flee, 17 avoided rape (81%).

Physical Resistance:
Thirty out of 40 avoided rape (75%).

Yelling or Screaming:
Twenty-five out of 40 avoided rape (63%).

Cognitive Verbal Techniques:
Thirty-six out of 67 avoided rape (54%).

Pleading:
Eleven out of 25 avoided rape (44%).

Of the five strategies, pleading was the most ineffective

Of the five strategies, pleading was the most ineffective and most frequently associated with being raped. The most often used strategy for avoiders appears to have been a combination of screaming [yelling] and use of physical resistance. Moreover, avoiders were more likely to use multiple strategies. The most frequent number of strategies used was three for avoiders *versus* only one for raped women.

> Environmental Intervention
>
> Outside intervention occurred in 12 of the 94 cases; in 10 of these, the effect was to thwart the rape attempt.
>
> No Strategies
>
> The five women who made no attempt to resist were all raped. Outside intervention constitutes external forces. These external forces can only be attributed to luck and cannot be counted on.
>
> Physical Resistance and Injury
>
> Bart found no relationship between the women's use of physical resistance and the rapists' use of additional force over and above the rape attempt. In fact, she states that "...sexual assault does not usually result in serious physical injury and that physical resistance often results in minor injury such as bruises and scratches. ... Not resisting is not a guarantee that no injury will occur."[20]

Lita Furby and Baruch Fischhoff reviewed 24 studies of the effectiveness of possible self-defense strategies.[21] The objective of their review was to clarify sometimes conflicting conclusions emerging from these studies—conflicts caused by the difficulty in collecting data, by the lack of consistency among studies, and by the problem of extracting general lessons from the myriad of possible self-defense strategies. Nevertheless, with all the limitations of the studies, Furby and Fischhoff found that the results generally converged—for both individual and categories of strategies.

They classified statistically significant categories as either harmful or effective.

Harmful Strategies

All five of the strategies listed below were intended to reduce or minimize the assailant's propensity to rape, but they did not:

Cooperation

Noncooperation without resistance

Making a moral appeal

Crying

Reasoning

Strategies That Are Effective

The three individual strategies listed below showed clear evidence of being effective in reducing the assailant's propensity to rape:

Yelling

Fleeing/running

Resistance with physical force

Multiple Strategies

Furby and Fischhoff found that the more tactics the individual used, the greater the chance of avoiding rape.

The authors summarized their findings: "...There appears to be consistent evidence that the more assertive or forceful strategies tend to be effective in avoiding rape, in contrast to the less forceful ones, which seem ineffective or perhaps even somewhat harmful. Moreover, the same pattern of differential harm and benefit emerged not only within individual studies, but also across different types of studies."[22]

What Strategies Are Effective if the Assailant Has a Weapon?

Few studies have compared the effectiveness of self-defense strategies when the assailant does and doesn't have a weapon. Furby and Fischhoff note that "...fewer women may resist when weapons are present—but when they do, that resistance is apparently often effective in avoiding rape."[23]

One study (McDermott), in studying assaults by strangers with weapons, found the following: resisting was associated with a 52% greater chance of avoiding rape than not resisting. Seventy percent of those who did not resist were raped, while a much smaller number, 18%, of those who resisted were raped.[24]

Black and Skogan surveyed the role of weapons and nonforceful resistance in stranger rapes. When a weapon was present, resistance increased the chances of avoiding rape by 43% to 53%.[25]

Browne and Beyeler found that fighting was effective, but it was somewhat less so when the assailant had a weapon. These researchers found screaming to be slightly less effective when a weapon was present. Talking significantly increased avoidance chances when a weapon was present but not when there was no weapon.[26]

Bart found that the presence of a weapon was not the main factor differentiating rape from rape avoidance.[27]

Rape Defense and Avoidance Strategies—Stranger Attacks

I believe that active resistance is the best means of

avoiding rape. The concept of active resistance takes into account psychological and preventive measures as well as physical defense.

Your best defense is to prevent an assault from occurring in the first place. You do this through a combination of psychological and active preventive measures which will keep distance between you and a potential assailant. The preventive measures involve physical/mechanical security as well as your personally taking part in their implementation (See Chapter 8—Keeping Your Personal Power on the Streets.)

If prevention fails or breaks down and if you are confronted with the possibility of an assault, you utilize the best possible strategies to thwart the assault.

What Strategies Are Effective?

The researchers generally agreed that multiple strategies work best. They also agreed that the more forceful strategies were most effective. Therefore, if attacked or threatened with attack, I advocate immediate forceful resistance. (See Chapter 2—The Psychology of Empowerment.) Immediately: get furious, yell ferociously, physically incapacitate the assailant (if necessary), and run!

What Strategies Are Ineffective or Even Harmful?

The less forceful strategies tended to be ineffective or even counterproductive. These include: pleading, no resistance, cooperation, and crying. Talking is not noticeably effective.

What if the Assailant Has a Weapon?

The researchers agreed that the outcome of the encounter is more determined by the actions and determination of the resister. The major concern of the women who avoided being raped was "determining not to be raped and fighting back."[28]

Although fewer women resist when a weapon is present, resistance does increase the chance of avoiding rape. Yet, guns and knives are lethal weapons. So then what we really need to discuss are your strategies if the assailant is armed. There is a big difference between someone pointing a knife at your throat or a gun against your head and someone with a gun or knife approaching you from the other side of a parking garage.

The first thing to remember is to be aware. Aware and alert body language will significantly reduce your chances of even being targeted and will prevent you from being taken by surprise.

Successful resistance is a combination of both psychological and physical techniques and tactics. It is most important for you to keep alert and keep your mind active. The woman who panics and freezes in a crisis situation is the one who will be victimized.

Your immediate goal is to escape. The best time to get away is when you have both an opportunity to do so and a place to go. Circumstances dictate your choice of resistance strategies. The assailant's immediate goal is to get you under his control. He also wants to get you to an area which is isolated so that he can do what he wants to you. This may include rape and or murder.

For example, if an assailant drives up to you, points a gun, and tells you to get into the car, I would strongly advise not to comply. Under no circumstances would I permit myself to get into a car with a rapist. If possible, turn in the opposite direction and run away. Suppose the assailant grabbed you, put a gun or knife to you, and told you to get in the car. My advice is still under no circumstances would I permit myself to get into a car with a rapist. Immediate, forceful physical resistance would not be the best strategy here. Other resistance strategies are available to you. My plan of resistance in this particular situation is a combination of deception followed by physical action, if the opportunity presents itself. I suggest feigning a faint. You simply pretend to pass out. If you have ever observed the police trying to carry off a protestor, you would notice that it takes several police officers to carry off a single limp demonstrator. If the rapist still wants to cart you off, he will have great difficulty trying to do so with one hand. Therefore, when you feel two hands on you, the gun isn't in his hands any longer and you will have your opportunity to immediately physically incapacitate him. (See Chapter 9—Physical Self-Defense.)

Under certain circumstances, it is extremely risky for you to try immediate, physical resistance. In a case that was reported to me, a woman was threatened in her home by a man who had gotten in through an unlocked door. He picked up a bayonet, which she happened to have in her apartment, and forced her to go into the bedroom. It was nighttime, in the summer. The windows were open, the shades open, and a bedroom light was turned on. He told her to lie down on the bed. She calmly did so. Thinking she was cooperating and under his control, the would-be rapist put the weapon down as he reached up to turn the light off. It was then that she seized her opportunity. As he was reaching for the light, she grabbed the bayonet and stabbed him in the back. Dripping with blood, he staggered out of the apartment.

It is extremely important to survey the situation and plan your actions. In the first instance, trickery was used; in the second, temporary cooperation. In both cases, the goal was the same. Wait for or create an opportunity to fight back physically and/or to get away.

If you are being attacked with a knife and cannot get away, resistance is your best option. Are You A Target? A Guide To Self-Protection and Personal Safety (by Dr. Judith Fein, Torrance Publishing Company) offers detailed instructions and photographs in defense against knife attacks. (Are You A Target?... is available through a bookstore, or you may use the order form at the end of this book.)

Research on Rape Defense and Avoidance Strategies—Known Assailant

What is the difference in effectiveness of strategies if the victim/resister and assailant know each other? Furby and Fischhoff found that in general the pattern of results is quite similar for the two types of assailants: the less forceful strategies tended to be harmful, whereas the more forceful ones tended to be effective in avoiding rape.

However, there are three notable differences between the stranger and acquaintance data: (1) crying was classified as harmful in a stranger situation, but not harmful with acquaintances; (2) reasoning was classified as harmful in a stranger situation, but not harmful with acquaintances; (3) resistance with force was more effective with strangers than with acquaintances.[29]

Levine-MacCombie and Koss studied the effectiveness of avoidance strategies in acquaintance rape. They found the active strategies (running away and screaming for help) more successful than cognitive strategies (reasoning, pleading, crying, quarreling, turning cold). Quarreling with the offender contributed significantly to the prediction of completed rape. In this study, physical resistance was not found to differentiate victims from avoiders.[30]

In summary, the researchers found that the more active resistance strategies were more effective, while the passive strategies tended to be harmful. More studies in the area of acquaintance rape resistance need to be conducted. Very few exist. The question of the effectiveness of physical resistance needs to be researched further. My concern is that the research did not consider the question of whether or not the subjects studied had self-defense training. Given the scarcity of self-defense training in the general population of women, it is not surprising that the women who were assaulted did not know how to respond effectively either physically or psychologically. The issue of rape and the acquaintance or known assailant is so pervasive that it merits further discussion. (See Chapter 5—Acquaintance Rape Avoidance and Defense.)

What Research Tells Us

In contrast to traditional advice, research into rape avoidance and resistance tells us unquestionably that passive resistance, pleading, and cooperation with the rapist are not only ineffective but also harmful and lead directly to rape. The message to us is loud and clear: immediately and forcefully resist!

FIVE

ACQUAINTANCE RAPE AVOIDANCE AND DEFENSE

ACQUAINTANCE RAPE AVOIDANCE AND DEFENSE

Scope of the Problem

Acquaintance Rape is the Least Reported of All Sexual Assaults—Yet It Is the Most Pervasive

It accounts for 80 to 90 percent of all incidents.[31] In a survey of 6,159 women and men in institutions of higher learning throughout the United States, researcher Mary Koss found that 53.7% of the female respondents revealed some form of sexual victimization and that 25.1% of the male respondents had been involved in some form of sexual aggression. Moreover, since the age of fourteen, 27.5% of college women reported experiencing—and 7.7% of college men reported perpetrating—an act that fits the legal definition of rape. [32]

The legal definition of forcible rape, as defined by the U.S. Department of Justice, is "...the carnal knowledge of a female forcibly and against her will. Assaults or attempts to commit rape by force or threat of force are also included; however, statutory rape (without force) and other sex offenses are excluded." [33] This definition of forced sexual intercourse, which excludes oral or anal sex, is extremely limited. The definition of sexual assault is more encompassing. The definition of sexual assault as found in the California Penal Code is "any involuntary sexual act in which a person is threatened, coerced, or forced to comply against his/her will." [34]

Diana Russell interviewed 930 women who were 18 years or older. [35] Dr. Russell used the conservative definition of forcible rape (above) so as to be able to compare her findings with those of government statistics. Forty-four percent of the individuals in Russell's study had been the victim of rape or attempted rape; of these, 89% of the assailants were known to the victims. Fifty percent had been raped more than once. Only 10% of the women who said that they had been raped had reported the crime to the police.

The National Victim Center of Arlington, Virginia, and The Crime Victims Research and Treatment Center of Charleston, South Carolina, released a survey in April 1992, based on 4,008 female respondents.[36] The survey estimated that there were 683,000 forcible rapes committed against women 18 or older. The study confirmed the disturbing fact reported by Dr. Russell: most rapes were committed by known assailants—67% in this case—31% by acquaintances and 36% by relatives. Only 22% were committed by strangers.

Government figures don't even touch the tip of the iceberg. The Bureau of Justice Statistics, which produces the National Crime Survey, reported only 130,000 attempted and completed rapes in 1990.[37] The FBI's Uniform Crime Reports stated that only 102,560 rapes were reported to the police in 1990.[38] Why are government figures so low? One explanation is that the FBI's Uniform Crime Reports includes only rapes reported to the police. The closer the relationship of the victim to the rapist, the less likely it is that the crime will be reported. Secondly, the scope of reporting is very narrow: only the legal definition of forcible rape is counted. The real number of occurrences is probably ten to fifteen times greater than the government reports.[39]

Societal Attitudes

We have a problem of epidemic proportions. Consider the following:

- Sixty percent of college aged-men said they would commit a rape if they know they could get away with it.[40]
- A 1987 survey in Rhode Island schools showed

that one in four middle-school boys thought it was O.K. to force a girl to have sex if he spent more than $10 on her. [41]

- Rape is the only brutal crime for which the public frequently blames the victim.
- Most rape victims blame themselves for the rape.
- No more than 5 percent of reported rapes actually results in conviction.[42]

A seventeen year-old girl went with her boyfriend to a friend's home. She consumed some alcohol and went into the bedroom with him. Three of his friends came into the bedroom and wanted to have group sex with her. She objected. This young woman was gang raped by 4 teen-age boys.[43]

We are living in a society in which the victim is blamed for being a victim, in which many men would commit a rape if they could get away with it, in which most men who are arrested for rape are never convicted, and in which boys think that sex is due them if they spend money on a date.

Special Issue: Campus Rape

The magnitude of acquaintance rape and the shocking reality of its widespread practice can be found on college campuses. The typical victim is a freshman and the typical rape is committed during the first few weeks of the school year. This is when the experience of going away to college is new. Many young women are naive, have never been away from home before, and are disoriented: unfamiliar location, many strangers, feeling alone and isolated. What easy prey they make. "...the upperclassmen are waiting for them. They know how to manipulate the girls, know what they can get away with, what they should say, what moves to make."[44]

The vast majority of these rapes go unreported. They are

largely ignored by students, parents, and college administrators. It is a problem that college administrators would prefer to sweep under the rug and one which parents would prefer to deny. Since very few incidents are reported, many times a reported rape is treated as a shocking, isolated event. If parents believe the stereotype that the typical campus rape is committed by a lone stranger, then the easy answer would be campus security. If the parents believed that the few reported incidents were date rapes, that the victim could be blamed because she had been drinking, or that the victim had in any way acted imprudently, then the parents didn't have to worry about their own "virtuous" daughters.

Sometimes, in response to rape scares and the myth that most rapes are committed by strangers, "Don't walk alone" campaigns and student escort services are initiated. Why should a young woman trust her escort? Do women have more to fear from someone who might jump out of the bushes and drag them off or from the men that usher them to their residence halls? Dolores Card, program director of the Rape Crisis Center of Syracuse states that "Seventy-five percent of adult rapes that come to my center are acquaintance rapes, usually committed in the victim's home; on college campuses, the percentage is even higher."[45]

The Federal Government, through the Campus Security Act, is now requiring all universities and colleges to provide student, faculty, staff, and prospective students with crime statistics for the previous three years, as well as a description of security procedures. Schools that don't comply risk losing eligibility for federal money.[46] Although this is a step in the right direction, assaults reported to campus police only cover the campus and not the area close to the campus where many students live. As is corroborated in other rape statistics, very few actual rapes are reported to the police. For example, the

University of Iowa police reported four sexual assaults in one year; yet during the same time period, the Victim Advocacy Program handled 39 rapes.[47]

To their credit, some colleges and universities have implemented sexual assault policies. San Francisco State University's detailed Sexual Assault Policy states that: "...The University will not tolerate acts of sexual assault. All reported instances of sexual assault will be investigated and appropriate disciplinary, criminal, and/or legal action will be taken, with the consent of the victim. Appropriate support services will be made available to students, faculty, or staff who are victims of sexual assault." [48] The policy goes on to detail: (1) implementation, responsibilities, and services (case managers, university police, housing and residential services, student health services, counseling and psychological services, etc.); (2) sexual assault prevention programs (ongoing sexual assault education and prevention programs to: residence hall students, advisors, athletic teams, fraternities and sororities, and other groups), and (3) disciplinary sanctions.

San Francisco State University created The S.A.F.E. Place which is a resource center for information, crisis counseling, and referral for sexual harassment and sexual assault. I spoke with Nina Jo Smith, the center's director, who stated that, with the support of the Dean of Student Affairs, the program has been very successful. In the first nine months of 1992, over 50 individuals came in for assistance; in contrast, only 1 to 2 rapes were reported to the campus police.

Special Issue: Athletes and Rape

Psychologist Chris O'Sullivan of Bucknell University studied 26 gang rapes that were documented between 1980 and 1990 and found that fraternity groups and athletic teams committed the highest number of rapes. [49] As with any acquaintance rape, reporting and conviction rates are very low. Female victims are laden with shame, humiliation, and campus pressure to drop the charges. Over 90 percent don't press charges. [50] Most college women are so devastated that they drop out of school.[51]

The roots of this practice go very deep into male traditions and the male belief system. Men who commit acts of gang rape don't feel guilty, believe the victim had it coming to her, and don't even consider it rape. What makes athletes so special and what makes teams, in particular, believe that they are outside of the law? One clue may be the dynamics of the team experience itself. Gang rape is not commonly found among athletes who participate in individual sports. Athletes on football, basketball, and hockey teams, for example, are most prone to group rape. Athletes who work and play together become deeply bonded. These men develop a "powerful subculture founded on aggression, privilege and the scapegoating of women."[52] According to Dr. Sullivan, sports foster a supermasculine attitude in which aggression is connected with sexuality.[53] For these athletes, sex is only satisfying if it is a conquest. The pressure to "score" is enormous. Men tend to talk about scoring on and off the field as if it were the same thing.

Consider the following Associated Press report: "Lawyers for a Spokane woman...released the names of 20 current and former Cincinnati Bengals accused in a civil lawsuit of raping her or standing by while she was assaulted nearly two years ago. ...the plaintiff, described as a 98 pound mother of four, was brutally and sadistically raped...over two hours, by 13 to 15 Bengal players who were two to three times her size, on the 'team floor' of a Seattle hotel on October 3, 1990, when the team was in town to play the Seahawks. ... Despite her pleas for help and mercy, these players assaulted and battered the plaintiff by forcibly committing repeated acts of carnal intercourse and physical abuse. ..."[54]

In many cases, athletes view their victim as different from other women: cheap, a slut, a whore. Many believe that if she said "No" she really meant "Yes." They may have heard that she was "easy"—perhaps because a teammate had already slept with her.[55] Once a woman is put into this category, she is dehumanized—an object, not a human being. Therefore, it is O.K. to attack her. The same type of thinking was used by American soldiers in the Vietnam War at the My Lai gang rape and massacre. It is O.K. if they are not human beings like us.

Athletes are adored by the public, who consider them superheroes. Special privileges are afforded to star athletes. The male stars attract constant female adoration. They also receive college scholarships, lots of support, and attention. Star teams bring campuses and communities money and notoriety. Oftentimes the entire community comes to the support of the team, and juries are very lenient.

Anatomy of a Gang Rape

The victim is alone or can be separated from her friends; she is drinking or tricked into drinking alcoholic beverages; she is friendly, perhaps flattered with attention given her by a member or members of the team; she may have had a prior sexual relationship with a member of the team. The woman is given alcohol to drink and is led into an area in which she is isolated from her friends or where she is alone with team members.

She is gang raped or sodomized. The perpetrators are insensitive to her pleas or cries. Male bonding is what is all-important here. They take turns sexually assaulting her, at the same time, cheering each other on. Those that do not participate watch or take videos. No one tries to stop the rape.

The men believe the woman "asked for it," "deserved it,"

and they have no guilt or remorse. They don't feel they raped their victim, whom they consider a "slut" or "tramp." They maintain their code of silence and are supportive of teammates.

Team members are rarely prosecuted. If prosecuted, they are rarely convicted. They receive support and encouragement from the home town, and their actions are mitigated or not taken seriously by the legal system.

Acquaintance Rape Avoidance and Defense Strategies

An attack by an acquaintance has different dynamics than one committed by a stranger. By understanding the circumstances surrounding this type of rape, we can prepare to prevent or counter it.

Acquaintance Rape Methodology—"Come into my parlor said the spider to the fly."

The known assailant is likely to use entrapment to corner his prey. His game plan is to maneuver his victim to an area where she is alone with him and where he is not likely to be discovered. It is also a situation in which she is not likely to be believed—"What were you doing alone in his apartment?", or "You invited him in didn't you?" He then may either suddenly attack or begin a progressive assault which is usually perceived as a sexual advance in the initial stages. At this point, the woman still believes that she has a choice and that her wishes will be respected. Although she may have felt apprehension, she discounts her own feelings. She may protest, but her "No's" will go unheeded. Many times the rapist denies that he has sexually assaulted his victim. After all, they were playing a game—he scored and she lost. What a poor sport!

Prevention Strategies

How do you prevent acquaintance rape without compromising the quality of your life? Can you go out on dates or go to parties? Can you go to a fraternity party or to a party thrown by the local football team to celebrate their latest victory? Or suppose a man that you met at a dinner party offers you a ride home? Should you accept his offer?

One of the most important skills that you need to develop is the skill of trusting your intuition—the ability to heed your instinct and react accordingly. If you feel that something is wrong, <u>something is wrong</u>! Why don't many women listen to their sixth sense? So-called "women's intuition" is held in low regard by the society—just as is anything relegated to the realm of women, such as housework and raising children. Intuition cannot be quantitatively measured. Many successful male leaders use intuition in decision-making. They just don't call it intuition—they call it a hunch. Learning to trust your instinct is the most basic and important of all prevention/avoidance strategies.

Whether or not you go out on a date or go to a party is a matter of choice. Personal power implies choice. What you must change is your level of awareness, and you must stay in control. Understand the entrapment game, and refuse to play it. How do you maintain control? You maintain control of your environment as well as your choices.

Traditional dating, for example, is set up to favor the male power structure. He is completely in control and his date is completely dependent. He picks her up, provides the transportation—even opening the car door for her, pays for dinner, and pays for entertainment. She is nicely, or even seductively, dressed—which is how society has influenced her to dress to please her date. In many cases, she is wearing high heels (which may restrict her movement.) She is polite, listens all evening to what her date has to say, smiles and is friendly. After all, isn't this what the female is instructed to do on a date? She has been taught to believe that she does not owe him anything. Yet she has not controlled her environment and has put herself into a potentially isolated situation. Can she trust this man? Does he expect sex at the end of the evening? Many do and many believe that they have paid for it. If she does not consent, it is rape.

My best advice is not to get into an isolated situation with anyone, unless you know him well enough to fully trust him. The initial stages of dating are times when you try to get to know another person. Do you want someone whom you do not know very well to know where you live? Do you want to drive off in a stranger's car? Why not meet in a public place? Provide your own transportation or carry enough money for taxi fare home. You can also pay for part of the date. Above all, listen to your gut feelings. Is he interested in you or what you have to say, or is he only interested in himself and his exploits? What does he have to say about women? What words does he use?

Suppose a man that you met at a dinner party offers you a ride home? He seem nice and friendly. He has a good job and perhaps you a looking for a new male friend. And after all, he is the friend of your friend. Doesn't that make him "safe"? Hardly!

If I did not know him well enough to trust him, I certainly wouldn't accept his ride. However, if you say "No," maybe you will never see him again. If that is the case, you wouldn't want to see him again anyway. What if you say "No," and he pressures you? Then you certainly wouldn't want to see him again. How do you say "No"? You say "No" directly—with your eyes, your voice, and your body language.

Rape Avoidance and Defense Strategies—Graduated Responses

Suppose you are in an isolated situation with an acquaintance. If your intuition tells you that something is wrong, then you must pay attention—even if you feel only mildly uncomfortable. Susan Smith, who conducted a four-part survey on rape and rape resistance states that "Delayed-threat perception and delayed-effective response are the greatest contributing factors to successful known-assailant rapes." In fact, 59 percent of the women raped by known-assailants in Smith's survey reported being pinned down with the man's body weight holding them down.[56] It is very important for you to read the assailant's signals and to take immediate action before he physically attacks.

The assailant does not want to be caught in the act of raping. I would suggest commanding him to stay away. Be direct and forceful and loud. Say, "Don't take one step closer," or "Stop," or "Don't touch me," or something similar. Remember to look directly into his eyes and to use clear, consistent verbal signals, as well as direct body language.

If he doesn't stop, then you need to be more aggressive. Here, just as with the stranger rapist, you must get angry and furious. Yell at him to get away from you and to leave you alone. At this point, you may wish to create a very loud, noisy scene. Remember, the acquaintance rapist does not want to be caught. Moreover, he doesn't want evidence of a fight to be found. So, throw things around the room—dishes, ashtrays, lamps—anything that leaves a mess.

If the situation precludes physical resistance or if you are pinned down, I would suggest feigning. I learned this concept in fencing. You literally trick the assailant into believing one thing, and then you do something else. You can only do this if you keep your mind functioning clearly and keep telling yourself that you are going to stop him and get away safely. One example of a ruse is to tell him that you need to use the bathroom or you wish to freshen up. Once you are out of his physical control, you may be able to escape.

If the situation worsens and if you need to fight back

physically, then do so. Remember, this man is trying to rape you. By doing so, he intends to rob you of your dignity and self-determination. He has no right to do this. You do whatever you need to do to preserve you integrity as a human being. (Physical resistance is described in Chapter 9— Physical Self-Defense.)

SIX

SEXUAL HARASSMENT AND DISCRIMINATION IN THE MILITARY

A Personal Journey Toward Empowerment

SEXUAL HARASSMENT AND DISCRIMINATION IN THE MILITARY
A Personal Journey Toward Empowerment

Sexual Harassment and Discrimination in the Military

A young Army enlisted woman, Alxis Martinez Colon, suffered emotional distress as a result of being sexually harassed by her supervisors. According to reports, one sergeant ran his fingers through her hair and repeatedly kissed her cheek. Another asked if she had ever had sex with two men. She was pressured by the men who had harassed her not to report them. Yet, on April 27, 1992, Colon filed a formal complaint. The result: she was accused by the Army of being "guilty of conduct unbecoming a soldier."[57] Colon committed suicide.

On October 1, 1992, ABC's Primetime Live T.V. program reported on sexual abuse and discrimination of women in the military.[58] After interviewing many women veterans and women in military families, they concluded that sexual abuse occurred with alarming frequency within the military establishment. Statistics either were not kept or were grossly inadequate. The services did not even have a uniform reporting system. What was more alarming to me was the social process involved. The women not only were not believed but also were treated as if they were the criminals, rather than the victims. Often, a woman who reported being sexually assaulted was interrogated, was forced to take a polygraph test, and then was told she was a liar. The military conspired to cover up the cases; the "old boys" closed ranks and protected each other. Only recently—

after Anita Hill courageously took her stand on sexual harassment—have women forged together, unwilling any longer passively to accept abuse and discrimination.

The Tailhook Incident

On September 6, 1991, at the Tailhook Association convention in Las Vegas, twenty-six women were forced down a gantlet of male drunken, abusive naval aviators. The Marine and Navy pilots, grabbed at the females' breasts and crotches. In some cases, the women were disrobed. The Navy covered up the investigation. This time, the women didn't take it lying down. Lieutenant Paula Coughlin blew the whistle and went public.[59]

An independent probe of the Navy's response to the sex scandal has shaken the service to its very core. Top Naval officers have been forced to retire, 175 officers face disciplinary action, and the Navy has been forced to confront this problem. Acting Navy Secretary Sean O'Keefe told a press conference, "Our senior leadership is totally committed to confronting this problem and demonstrating that sexual harassment will not be tolerated—and those who don't get the message will be driven from our ranks."[60] This will be true only if women keep up their diligence and refuse to tolerate incidences of sexual harassment.

A Personal Journey

"I, Judith Fein, Captain, Military Intelligence, hereby tender my unqualified resignation as a Reserve Officer of the [United States] Army...

"I am submitting this resignation because I can no longer be a party to an organization which on one hand publicly expounds...equal opportunity for women, while on the other hand continues its blatant and insidious policies of sex discrimination. In my eleven years as a[n] ... Army officer I have never seen or perceived equal...treatment for women. The Army traditionally has been an all-male preserve. Advancement and survival is based on being a member of the 'old boys network'—a network of informal relationships with fellow team members from which women are excluded. Women...are expected to play supportive, nonaggressive, differential roles. Any assumption of control or leadership by a woman, especially over men, is upsetting to the men. A female superior (as well as subordinate) must gently and indirectly 'suggest' or 'question' but not command men.

"... I cannot in good conscience remain in the Army Reserve—in an organization in which I can see no future for me or for other women... ."[61]

I joined the Army and went on active duty in 1966. I endured many years of blatant sexual discrimination and sexual harassment both on active duty until 1970 and in the Reserves until 1977 when the situation became intolerable and I resigned my commission. I have been asked why I gave up the lucrative benefits of a military career. All I would have had to do would have been to stay in the military for less than nine more years.

People ask me why I teach self-defense for women. Although I have never been raped, I am frequently asked that question. In order for me to write this chapter on sexual harassment, I have had to examine my own past. A striking parallel exists between my own self-examination and the process that many of my self-defense students have gone through during the course of learning self-defense. They remember the past. By the process of self-discovery, they heal whatever hurt occurred—be it one, ten, or twenty years ago—and for the first time gain power and control over their lives. They gain their freedom, and with this freedom, experience both an immense sense of relief and the "joie de vivre."

I have been stating for years that the reason why I instruct women in self-defense is because it is my goal to empower women. Just as many other women have been, I have been assaulted by acquaintances and by strangers on the street. I have succeeded in fighting them off. My process of self-discovery has led me to remember what I have buried in my past—the U.S. Army attempted to psychologically rape me and succeeded in psychologically abusing me. I fought back and won—at great emotional cost to myself; I felt forced to resign my commission—feeling that I could no longer honorably serve my country.

I was commissioned in the military before the Women's Movement of the 1970's began. I wanted adventure and excitement—to be stationed in France and to tour Europe at my leisure. This was not to be. During Officers' Training School, I took the initiative to meet with the head of Military Intelligence (MI) Training at the Pentagon. The colonel agreed to send me to Counterintelligence School. Because I did not go through the chain of command and because I did not accept a desk job reading surveillance maps, I was "punished" by being stationed in a "hardship" area—Korea. Before I was shipped off to Korea, I attended Intelligence Officer School at Fort Holibird, Maryland.

Needless to say, I was the only female in the class. It was at this school that I was not only sexually harassed, but escaped a rape attempt by a fellow officer—a Green Beret. The rape attempt left me feeling frightened. The lieutenant promised to come back and finish what he started. I purchased a .38 caliber pistol which I knew how to use since I had been a member of the Sixth Army Pistol Team in my previous assignment. Although the Green Beret did not attempt to assault me sexually again, the threat was still there, and I had to see him every day.

One incident of sexual discrimination which stands out in my mind occurred when the class was assigned to field training—three days of going into the woods to play spy and counterspy. The boys did not want their games spoiled by the presence of a female. The class commander told me that there were no "facilities" in the field for women (no "lady's room")— the gents, I deduced from my intelligence reports, used the bushes—and that I would have to stay behind to work in the office. I protested, to no avail. I did not have any recourse. I refused to stay back at the office while the "boys" were out playing war games. I left the post—completely contrary to orders and military regulations. I told the class commander that I would be back when the rest of the class returned. I returned, feeling excluded and not a part of the team.

Every other (male) officer who had attended Intelligence School with me and who went to Korea was assigned to a field position. I was assigned to the MI Battalion Headquarters—the only woman assigned to the unit. The Executive Officer, a lieutenant colonel, called me into his office and told me that he didn't approve of women in the military. This arrogant representative of the U.S. Military stated that, if it were up to him, he would not have any army women in Korea and certainly not in his battalion! To my knowledge, the word "sexual harassment" had not yet been coined.

I arrived in Korea in the dead of winter—December of 1967—and was quartered in a facility about two miles from Battalion Headquarters. Every morning, the battalion sergeants picked up the male officers, by jeep, at their quarters and took them to work. In a blatant display of sexual harassment, our sergeants refused to pick me up. Their excuse was that my quarters were out of the way. It was cold. Having no other form of transportation, I was forced to walk the two miles, many times in the snow. A couple of months later, I arranged to have a motorcycle imported from Japan. A friend, Peter, taught me how to ride. Every morning, on schedule, the sergeants picked up the male officers at their quarters. I, wearing my combat fatigues and combat boots, rode to work on my motorcycle. I arrived prior to my scheduled shift, changed my clothing, and donned my approved uniform—a military suit which consisted of a skirt and jacket. I was reprimanded for riding a motorcycle and wearing fatigues and was requested to change my behavior. Since the sergeants refused to pick me up, I had no other means of transportation. I was entirely within my rights; I refused.

The only authorized place I could have my meals was in the officer's club. The dinnertime entertainment at the club consisted entirely of consuming very inexpensive alcohol, socializing with the "local women," or playing the slot machines. Out of disgust, I sought out the gymnasium. It was there that I spent my free time for the next year, going 5 or 6 evenings a week and fighting a Korean male black belt to earn my own black belt in Tae kwon do.

Two other incidences of sexual harassment stand out in my mind. The first of these occurred after I was promoted to captain (my promotion had come through after I had arrived from the States). A subordinate male officer told others that he would never work for a woman. He didn't have to. When my section chief was reassigned to the United States, I was the ranking officer in the section. Rather than allow a woman to command men, I was reassigned to a fancy-titled position, Plans Operations and Training Officer, which in reality was a major's job. The position called for a ranking major, one captain, one lieutenant, two sergeants and several enlisted men. This was a safe transfer for the battalion. I was the only one in the office and had to do everyone's job!

The second incident which comes to mind was during an alert. Several North Koreans had sneaked through our lines. The Eighth Army responded by a show of force. They cancelled all leaves, closed the base, and we donned our combat gear, complete with gas masks and pistols. I was assigned as the liaison officer between the MI Battalion and the Eighth Army Headquarters. Everything that was to go between headquarters and the battalion was to go through me. Again, sexual discrimination and sexual harassment prevailed. The boys formed their own informal network; I sat alone in my office until the crisis passed and we put our combat outfits away.

Shortly after this incident, the battalion received a request from a Korean general. The general asked to have someone teach English to his wife and to the wives of his staff officers. I had previously requested to be allowed to attend Korean language school. The Army refused, stating that I would never need to learn the language. Although I did not speak a word of Korean, our commanding officer chose me. At this junction, everything for me changed. Now I was told not to wear a uniform, so I didn't. Now I stopped riding my motorcycle to work. I did not have to. The Korean general sent a chauffeured limousine to the headquarters to pick me up. Imagine the look on the sergeants' faces. After several weeks, the general requested that I teach him English also. This was the beginning of a wonderful, mutually rewarding relationship among me, the general's family, and the general. I wish to state that the general was a perfect gentleman. I was treated with the utmost kindness and respect. I experienced not one hint of sexual harassment at the hands of the presumably patriarchal Koreans.

Toward the end of my tour of duty in Korea, I became involved in an incident which could have come out of a spy novel. The incident culminated in the U.S. Army attempting to discredit me and, by so doing, trying to destroy my career in the military as well as my self-esteem.

A package arrived from Hong Kong. I wasn't expecting anything, and did not know the name of the individual whose name was on the return address. Since I was suspicious, I opened this package in front of witnesses. The package contained expensive items. I suspected that this package had been sent to me by a Korean acquaintance, who then expected to collect the articles and avoid paying hefty customs duty. The previous month, the army had distributed a letter alerting all of us to the abuse of Army Post Office (APO) privileges. The APO's were being used to import merchandise intended for black market purposes. We were warned that "...Abuses of APO privileges may result in disciplinary action under the UCMJ [Uniform Code of Military Justice].[62]

I alerted my supervisor of the incident. He advised me to give the package to the Korean national. He advised me to commit an illegal action, which would have put me in a compromising position. I could not bring myself to do this. I took the package to the U.S. Army mail clerk. He advised me to refuse the package, remove my name, and return it to the sender. I did so.

The acquaintance called me and asked me if I had received a package. I told her that I returned it to the sender. She did not believe me and was very angry. She called me on the phone in the middle of the night ranting and raving that I was a liar and a thief and that she would make a lot of trouble for me. I slept that night with my .38 caliber pistol under my pillow.

The next morning, I informed my supervisor who informed the battalion commander. The Acting Commander (who was the same Executive Officer who had told me that he did not want or like women in the military) was furious with me. I was told that I had ruined relations with the Koreans. They put me under heavy security and told me that I would leave the country the next day—but not before I met again with the Korean general at a previously scheduled meeting. At the meeting, the general presented me with a special black belt which was inscribed with both our names, and gave me a wonderful letter: "...I would like to take this opportunity to extend my sincerest appreciation for the untiring efforts you have extended for the benefit of this Command during the past year. Your selfless enthusiasm has provided invaluable assistance to myself and key officers of my

Command. ...I wish you continued success and happiness...and assure you that we will long remember the young lady that helped us all so very much."[63]

My American supervisors attempted to punish me in typical Army fashion. They issued an adverse efficiency report. The report was in essence a character assassination. They wanted to punish me because I did not stay in my place and play their games. Now they had their chance to get back at the female who had "crashed" an all male preserve. They used words as weapons. I received low ratings in personal qualities although they did give me a high rating in moral courage. They also rated my job performance as low. They stated that I was uncooperative, that I was unable to command confidence or respect, and that I was not a team player. They recommended that I be reassigned to a Women's Army Corps basic training unit where I could teach physical fitness or karate. Not one word in this report mentioned or described my work with the general or discussed the incident with the Korean national that had embarrassed them. I felt that, if I left this personal attack unchallenged, my career in the military was over, and my record would be unfairly tarnished.

I came back to the United States and decided to fight back—and ran into a stone wall. I needed to gather evidence to support my story, so I wrote to people in Korea who knew me and who knew of the incident. I received no responses to my letters. I figured out that my mail was being intercepted and finally wrote to someone using a different name and return address. My letter got through. I collected statements and letters for almost a year and submitted a reclama (a document refuting their allegations). Because of overwhelming evidence, the Army backed down, and the adverse report was removed from my record.

I spent seven years in the Army Reserves after going off active duty. My involvement in the Reserves consisted of joining a unit, going to meetings one week-end a month, and serving two weeks a year on active duty. In a unit in Iowa, all the male officers took turns trying to see which one of them could get me into bed with him. Although none did, the work environment was at times charged with sexual connotations.

One summer, I was stationed at the Pentagon in Washington, D.C. Since I was in a counterintelligence unit, some days we wore uniforms and some days we didn't. On the days I wore a uniform, I was treated like anyone else. On the one day I put on a civilian summer dress, the men couldn't seem to keep their eyes off of me or specific parts of my anatomy. They smiled and acted like little boy idiots—a female of the species was in their presence! The next day, I put my uniform back on and continued to wear it throughout the rest of my assignment. The gawking stopped.

Another summer, I was assigned to intelligence school at Fort Huachucha, Arizona. Previously at Fort Huachucha, I had stayed in a new facility, the BOQ—an air-conditioned modern building. This particular summer, as customarily would have been my option, I decided to stay off-post. After three days, the military decided to require all officers to stay on-post. They put me in an old, non air-conditioned, co-ed barracks. I objected, and requested to stay at the BOQ. (Remember, Fort Huachucha was located in the southern part of Arizona and it was the middle of the summer.) They refused. Their reason was pure, unadulterated sexual harassment. They told me that since women wanted to be treated equally, they were going to treat them more than equally. I could stay in the barracks! I complained all the way up to the Inspector General—to no avail.

A final barrage of sexual harassment caused me to resign my commission. I was assigned to an intelligence unit in the San Francisco Bay Area. In this section of the unit, I was the ranking officer. According to military regulations and customs, I should have been the section chief. But this was not to be. I was pressured into a subordinate position by the unit commander. Their reasoning: since all the other members of the section were men, they would feel more comfortable with a male section leader. This was a humiliating position to be in. One evening, I drove my car to an officers' meeting at the unit. My brakes caught fire as I was exiting the freeway. I needed a ride back to San Francisco. Not one officer in the unit would help me. I was not a member of the team; I was totally alone.

The message I had been getting all along was that I, a female officer, was not wanted in the military—especially in Military Intelligence. It had taken me many years to understand that I personally was not the cause of the problem. I was not stupid, I was not weak, I was not a member of some subspecies. The military had tried to rob me of my self-respect, my self-esteem, and my dignity.

How, then, did I keep my sanity, self-esteem, and sense of hope? Paralleling the negativity, I took actions to affirm my positive qualities. I didn't let the Army beat me down. In Korea, for example, when the sergeants picked up the male officers and refused to give me a ride, I provided my own transportation. Moreover, I learned to drive a jeep and received a jeep driver's license. Whenever I chose, I drove a jeep myself. Even though this was considered "unladylike," there was very little anyone could do about it (since I outranked all of the sergeants.) I went on to affirm myself by earning a black belt in Karate from the Korea Tae kwon do Ji Do kwon Association—a worthy accomplishment. Although I was ignored as a liaison officer by the U.S. Army, I was praised by the Korean general for my liaison accomplishments. When I chose to leave active duty, immediately after the adverse report was removed from my record, I went on to earn my Ph.D. in Exercise Physiology and Physical Education. In 1977, I finally resigned my commission because

I had come to realize that it was time to "cut bait." I could not effectively work within the system. I could, however, work outside of the system, empowering women.

SEVEN

SEXUAL HARASSMENT
Shattering The Glass Pyramid

SEXUAL HARASSMENT
Shattering The Glass Pyramid

What is Sexual Harassment?

"Unwelcome sexual advances, requests for sexual favors, and other verbal or physical conduct of a sexual nature constitute sexual harassment when (1) submission to such conduct is made either explicitly or implicitly a term or condition of employment, (2) submission to or rejection of such conduct by an individual is used as the basis for employment decisions affecting such individual, or (3) such conduct has the purpose or effect of unreasonably interfering with an individual's work performance or creating an intimidating, hostile, or offensive working environment." [64] This is the Equal Employment Opportunity Commission's (EEOC) definition of sexual harassment.

The Glass Pyramid

"..Pyramids were symbols of the [male] sun god Amon-Ra. By its many passages and false chambers the pyramid was meant to house and protect the body, the treasures, and retinue of the Pharaoh..."[65]

The glass pyramid is an insidious icon of patriarchal oppression. It is the symbolic representation of a cultural machine designed to keep women at its base (repressed). Its purposes are (1) to keep women in their place and (2) to keep, and to protect, power and wealth in the hands of members of this cultural machine's fellowship. The fellowship wants success,

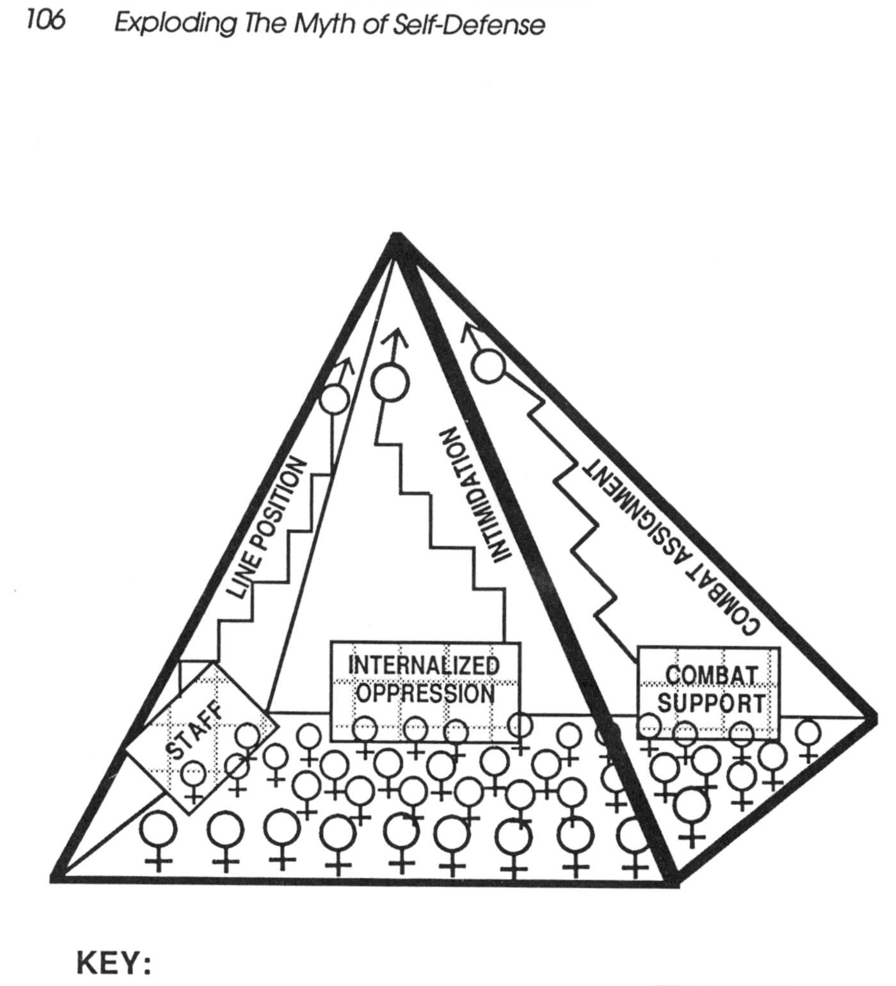

KEY:

Women's False Chambers

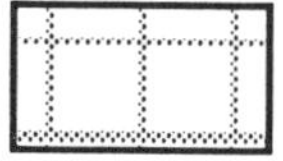

Men's Passages

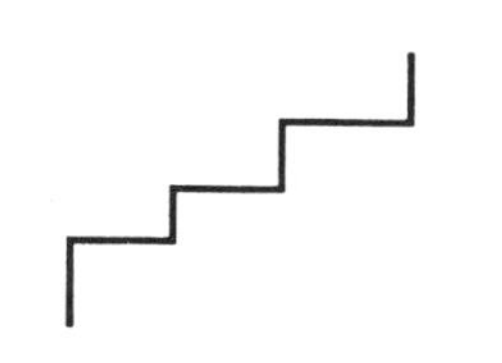

FIGURE 1. The Glass Pyramid

power, and wealth for itself and a handful of chosen males—who are, in essence, mirror images of itself, its values and its traditions.

Why the Pyramid Is Glass

The perpetuators of the pyramid are so self-assured that they believe that their glass is unbreakable. They are so arrogant that they discount the pyramid's vulnerabilities: glass can be seen through and glass can be shattered. Because of cultural conditioning, "victims" of the pyramid wouldn't dare to challenge or break it. Consider this analogy: the male sexual organs have long been used as the instrument and symbol of male power and aggression. Yet, the male genitalia, when exposed, are extremely weak and vulnerable. How can a rapist rape without exposing his genitals? Is he not afraid of having them torn asunder from his body? Not hardly. Patriarchal programming has so psychologically battered its female victims that all the rapist needs to do is an intimidation test prior to selecting his victim. If the potential victim can be intimidated, she will submit (see Chapter 2—The Psychology of Empowerment.) His genitals are safe, he can attack at will.

The pyramid system clearly discloses that there are few positions on the top, some in the middle, and many on the bottom. The bottom represents entry level, sub-entry, or unskilled positions. These jobs may be part time or hourly. Many carry few or no benefits. Needless to say, the pay is low. The top positions carry great power and wealth—control over decisions and other people, top compensations—wonderful perks! The further up you reach, the fewer and fewer choice positions there are; in fact, there are very few places on the top and many people that potentially might want in. It would be much easier to reach the top if 50% or more of the competition (women) were eliminated.

False Chambers and Many Passages of the Pyramid

How are women kept out? One method is to legislate laws which make it impossible for women to reach its highest levels. For example, in the military, combat experience is considered essential for promotion to the top positions. Women, by tradition, law and military regulation, have been excluded from combat occupational specialities and are put into combat support positions (a false chamber). (This chamber, however, appears to be breaking down as some combat roles are being opened to women .) A second example of this practice, used in many corporations, is to employ women in staff positions (false chamber) which are advisory, as opposed to line positions which carry authority. Staff positions, such as Fitness Director or Training Manager, do not contribute to the bottom line of corporate profit and are, therefore, considered less important than the line positions, such as Sales Director or Marketing Manager. Line positions are considered necessary leadership training for advancement [passage to the top of the pyramid]. Another measure, used frequently in the Reagan administration, was to thwart the Equal Employment Opportunity Act of 1972. Faludi reports: "At the same time that the EEOC's [Equal Employment Opportunity Commission] sex discrimination files were overflowing, the Reagan administration was cutting the agency's budget in half and jettisoning its caseload . The year Reagan came into office, the EEOC had twenty-five active class-action cases; a year later, it had none ..."[66] (preventing women access to the passages and treasures in the pyramid). A fourth method is for a U.S. president to appoint judges to the Supreme Court which reflect his party's political views. This practice has long-lasting and far-reaching consequences. If the majority of justices in the Supreme Court are conservative, their decisions are also likely to be conservative. "Within ten days in June 1989, the U.S. Supreme Court rolled back two decades of landmark civil rights decisions in four separate rulings. The court opened the way for men to challenge affirmative action suits, set up new barriers that made it far more difficult to demonstrate discrimination in court with statistics, and ruled that a 1866 civil rights statute doesn't protect employees from discrimination that occurs after they are hired."[67] (More false chambers to keep women trapped at the bottom of the pyramid.)

An even more powerful method is more perfidious—cause women to do it to themselves, to self-destruct. This is what sexual harassment is all about—to intimidate women back into subservience. If a woman lacks in self-esteem, in self-respect, and in a strong belief in herself, she won't even try to succeed. Gloria Steinem, in her book Revolution From Within,[68] states that "the pyramid ... became the grid through which many cultures were to see the world for centuries: from a 'male-headed' household to corporate structures in which all authority flows from the top; from hierarchical classrooms to religions in which God's will is interpreted by a pope or ayatollah.... as a universal pattern with almost no alternatives, this paradigm limits us at best and destroys us at its worst. It turns most human interactions into a contest that only one or a few at the top can win, and it teaches us that there is a limited amount of self-esteem to go around; that some of us can only have it if others do not. ... It is a pattern so ingrained that we may consider it 'natural' and be unaware of its existence."[69]

In order for a woman to enter any of the scientific or financial professions, she must be proficient in mathematics. The Barbie Doll of 1992 says, "Math class is tough."[70] Many, many girls and women think that they are stupid in math. If you have created a set of beliefs about how difficult math is for you, math is, in essence, difficult for you. If you think you need a security guard to escort you to your car, then you believe that you cannot protect or take care of yourself. For many years, I have had a card posted in my office. It reads:

"Thinking"[71]

If you think you are beaten, you are;
If you think you dare not, you don't.
If you'd like to win, but think you can't,
It's almost a cinch that you won't.
If you think you'll lose, you've lost,
For out in the world we find
Success begins with a person's will—
It's all in the state of the mind.

If you think you are outclassed, you are;
You've got to think high to rise.
You've got to be sure of yourself before
You can ever win a prize.
Life's battles don't always go
To the stronger or faster one,
But sooner or later the one who wins
Is the one who thinks [s]he can.

Legal Decisions Affecting Sexual Harassment [72]

Sexual harassment is clearly against the law. In 1964, Title VII of the Civil Rights Act prohibited sexual discrimination at work. In 1972, Title IX of the Civil Rights Act prohibited sexual discrimination in education. In 1980 the EEOC defined sexual harassment. In 1980, in the *Continental Can v. Minnesota* court case, it was determined that an employer and/or organization is liable for sexual harassment and must take prompt action to correct the problem. In the 1982 court case of *Huebschen v. Wisconsin Department of Social Services,* it was determined that submission to sexual advances cannot be made a condition of employment and that an organization is liable for the actions of its supervisors. In 1986, in the *Meritor State Bank v. Vinson* court case, it was determined that sexual harassment is a form of sex discrimination under Title VII and that allowing an environment of sexual harassment is unlawful. In 1991, in *Ellison v. Brady*, the court ruled that a "reasonable woman" standard (i.e., if another woman were in her shoes) should be applied by juries and judges in considering sexual harassment cases. The *Robininson v. Jacksonville Shipyard Inc.* case in 1991 determined that posting pornographic material at work is a type of sexual harassment and creates a hostile environment. The Civil Rights Act of 1991 stated that a victim of sexual harassment can attempt to recover compensatory and punitive damages from his or her employer. In 1992, the Minnesota Court of Appeals decided that an employee need not complain at the time about sexual harassment on the job in order to sue later and collect damages from the employer.

Shattering the Glass Pyramid and the Wheel of Oppression

Although sexual harassment is clearly against the law, bringing charges to court is a step taken far down the line and, many times, only as a last resort. Law suits are time-consuming, emotionally draining, and costly, with many attorneys unwilling to take sexual harassment cases on a contingency basis. One respondent to an Inc. Magazine poll stated that his company's policies are "laughed at, unless you raise hell and hire a top-gun lawyer."[73]

We are caught in a bind. On one hand, sexual harassment is illegal; yet on the other, the person who reports sexual harassment risks putting herself through emotional, legal, and financial hell. However, to live with sexual harassment insures our continued oppression in the glass pyramid. In a Working Woman poll of over 9,000, many readers insisted that filing a complaint still amounts to "career suicide."[74] More than 60 percent of respondents said that they personally have been harassed. Only one out of four reported the harassment—the vast majority feeling that they cannot safely report a problem. Let us take some steps which are aimed at breaking the glass.

The Rape Continuum

Sexual harassment is on the same continuum as rape. If we understand rape patterns, then we can understand how to break up patterns of sexual harassment (See "The Anatomy of an Assault" in Chapter 2—The Psychology of Empowerment.) Sexual harassment and the rape continuum consist of verbal, visual, and physical harassment which include one or more of the following:

- Subtle sexual comments, jokes, remarks
- Animalistic sounds, grunts, and mockery
- Explicit sexual remarks
- Blatant degrading, belittling statements
- Degrading visual images of women
- Unwanted physical touching
- Pressure for sexual favors
- Threatening body language
- Physical interference with movement
- Grabbing breasts, buttocks
- Sexual assault

The Wheel of Oppression

Sexual harassment can also be thought of as a "Wheel of Oppression"—a tool of the patriarchy, used to build the glass pyramid, keep women at its base, and run over anyone who tries to climb the passages to the top. The hub of the wheel is that part in the center, around which all else revolves. Women are represented by the hub of the wheel. The wheel cannot exist without the hub, just as a pyramid cannot exist without its base. The spokes, which symbolize men, are implanted into the hub and depict sexual harassment. The spokes of sexual harass-

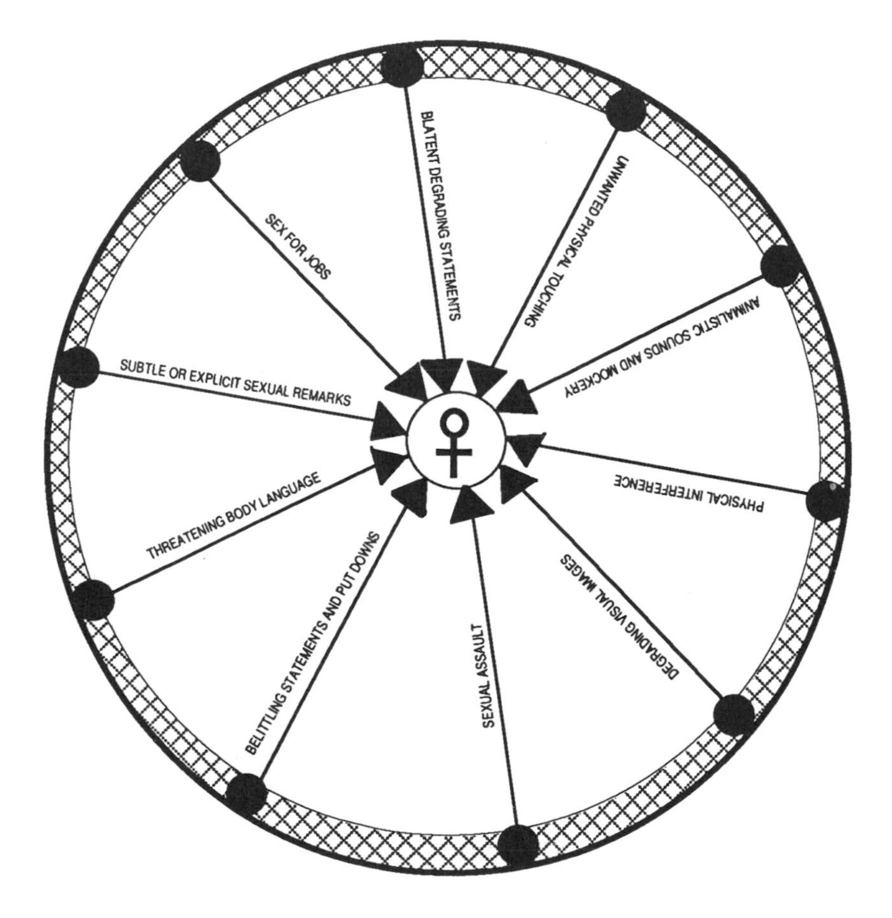

FIGURE 2. The Wheel of Oppression

ment hold the hub of the wheel in place, to keep the hub from moving out of its "designated" place. The wheel represents an instrument of torture and oppression to those at its hub and a weapon used to run over those women who attempt to pass upwards through the glass pyramid.

Nipping Sexual Harassment in the Bud

Just as a rapist targets his victim, so does the potential sexual harasser. Who will he target? If he is in a power position in the office, he may look for someone who needs the job—such as a single mother, someone who is young and innocent, or a subordinate who would like a promotion or a reference. Harassment becomes more likely as a woman rises in the corporate hierarchy—thus challenging the "all-male" domain. [75]

His next step is to test her to see if she can be intimated. If she can be intimidated, he will attack! The place to nip sexual harassment in the bud is in the testing phase. At this point the harasser has not developed a vested interest in the harassment—it is still a game. As yet, his ego is not very much involved. If stopped at this junction, a level of respect can be developed between the two of you, and you can continue working with him. If allowed to go further, he will develop a pattern of harassment. Any attempt to stop it will cause a loss of ego for him and may result in reprisals. I would suggest taking him aside and directly communicating to him that you will not permit, tolerate, or allow his behavior; that his behavior is unacceptable. Direct communication involves clear verbal instructions, assertive body language, and eye contact. All aspects of your communication mean the same thing: No is no, is no, is no! I believe that this is by far the best method. It takes high self-esteem, a belief in oneself, and a strong sense of anger and outrage. Earlier, in Chapter 3—Stories of Empowerment and Success, I related the story of Diane, the 98 pound, 4'11" woman who is the most "formidable person I know." I asked Diane what she would do if someone tried to sexually harass her. She replied, in no uncertain terms, "I'd tell them to get out of my face!"

Dismantling the Wheel

The next steps constitute a pattern of steps which are aimed at stopping the harassment or proceeding with grievances if the harassment has not been "nipped in the bud."

Informal Network.

If you have been harassed, chances are that the harasser is a recidivist—that he has harassed other women in the office. I suggest forming an informal network with other women co-workers. Call it anything you like—"the women's support group," "the women's reading group," or "the lady's sewing circle" Your "mission" is to exchange information on sexual harassment in the office. You need to know who is doing what to whom, when, where, and why. Meet on a regular basis and keep written records. You need to form a team—see who will support or join you in whatever action you choose to take. (If the hubs in the wheel cohere, they fuse together, thus immobilizing the wheel.)

Create a Nasty Scene.

If harassment persists, take the next available opportunity to embarrass the predator in front of the office staff. For example, if he grabs your breast, or rubs up against you, say very loudly, so that the whole office hears: "Get your filthy hands off me, you pervert! What would your wife and children say if they knew what you were doing!" Make sure there are plenty of witnesses. (Remove yourself (the hub) from the wheel—turn the game against him.)

Keep a Diary.

Record the nature, times, dates, and places of the objectionable conduct. Record you responses to the harasser, list names of witnesses, and any other pertinent information. (Collect evidence for your battle plan.)

Write a Letter to the Harasser.

Give him a factual account of the objectionable behavior. Then, express your thoughts that this type of conduct is unacceptable and that it is affecting your work performance. Tell him that you expect the behavior to stop so that you can continue to be productive on the job. Send the letter to him by certified mail, return receipt requested, keeping a copy for yourself. (Again, refuse to be a hub in the wheel of oppression.)

Formal Complaint.

If the above measures prove to be unsuccessful, then you have the option of filing a formal complaint. After the Thomas Supreme Court hearings in 1991 produced a charged atmosphere and after the Civil Rights Act of 1991 gave victims the right to sue for compensatory and punitive damages from their employers, companies scrambled to cover themselves. Many organizations now have written sexual harassment policies, with the aim of preventing workplace sexual harassment claims. For example, the California Labor Letter, in November 1991, stated: "The following are the *minimum* steps that employers should take in protecting their employees [as well as their own financial well-being]."[76] They should publish a written policy, provide training, and investigate all claims. Large companies have formal written sexual harassment policies. In a smaller company, complain to a senior-level person or the human resources person with responsibilities in this area. Make a formal appointment, make sure you are speaking to the correct person, and be very specific about your reasons for being there. Make it clear that you are keeping factual information about the incidents of harassment and that you expect the problem to be corrected.

Follow up with a confidential written report confirming the substance of your conversation. (You are going to break the wheel's spokes.)

Legal Action.

Although you may win large amounts of money in sexual harassment suits, suing for sexual harassment is comparable to a rape trial. Michael Green, an employment lawyer in San Francisco says that in litigation you must "brace yourself for the most far-flung attack on every aspect of your personal life."[77] Corporations, fearing loss, will do everything that they can to protect their assets. Even co-workers, whom you thought were your friends, may not even be willing to talk to you if they still work for the company. You must be willing to put up with all the abuse of a trial. Legal action is a fight. A powerful person picks her battles.

You shatter the glass pyramid by refusing to be a part of it. Personal power means control of your choices, control of your life—not permitting anyone to take away your integrity as a human being. Men practice sexual harassment to "keep you in your place." The little boys who have grown up to be "old boys" don't want to share. The little boys didn't want you to play and excluded you from playing on their teams. They did this so that they would be able to bond with each other and keep you from learning their secrets—of team play and cooperation. They preferred that you did not test your physical prowess, develop strength and, acquire an integration of mind and body. Now they want to keep you off the corporate team; or, if that is not possible, then they certainly don't want you to be the quarter-back.

Don't put up with it. Don't buy into it. If it gets to the point at which you have tried everything else to no avail, then if you choose to go to court, as I mentioned before, "... raise hell and hire a top-gun lawyer,"[78] and knock them off the seat of their pants—by so doing, you break the wheel of oppression.

François Millet, 19th Century French painter, who was influenced by social injustices prior to the French Revolution, created "The Man With A Hoe." Edward Markham, the American poet, after seeing Millet's painting, wrote in 1899 "The Man With The Hoe."[79] The parallels between the plight of the French peasant in 18th Century France and oppressed women is striking.

"Bowed by the weight of centuries he leans
Upon his hoe and gazes on the ground,
The emptiness of ages in his face
And on his back the burden of the world.
Who made him dead to rapture and despair...
A thing that grieves not and that never hopes...
Whose breath blew out the light within this brain?

"Is this the Thing the Lord God made and gave
To have dominion over sea and land;
To trace the stars and search the heavens for power;
To feel the passion of Eternity?
Is this the dream He dreamed who shaped the suns
And marked their ways upon the ancient deep?
Down all the caverns of Hell to their last gulf
There is no shape more terrible than this—
More tongued with censure of the world's blind greed—
More filled with signs and portents for the soul—
More packt with danger to the universe.

"What gulfs between him and the seraphim?
...what to him
Are Plato and the swing of Pleiades?
What the long reaches of the peaks of song,

The rift of dawn, the reddening of the rose?...
Through this dread shape humanity betrayed,
Plundered, profaned, and disinherited,
Cries protest to the Judges of the World,
A protest that is also prophecy.

"O Masters, lords and rulers in all lands,
Is this the handiwork you give to God...
How will you ever straighten up this shape;
Touch it again with immortality,
Give back the upward looking and the light;
Rebuild in it the music and the dream;
Make right the immemorial infamies
Perfidious wrongs, immedicable woes?..."

The cries of protest have become prophecy. When Anita Hill challenged President George Bush's appointment of Clarence Thomas to the Supreme Court, the welled-up dam burst. Even though Thomas' appointment was confirmed, the issues of sexism exploded across practically every television set, newspaper, radio station, and magazine in this country (as well as in the rest of the world). Women across every class, age, and ethnic boundary were profoundly affected. They also saw that they were grossly underrepresented in the U.S. Senate (2% female, 98% male) . Frustrated by a lack of power, and a lack of governmental attention to their special needs, women in this country became angry. This anger has united women and has forged the beginnings of a new and far-reaching change.

EIGHT

KEEPING YOUR PERSONAL POWER ON THE STREETS

KEEPING YOUR PERSONAL POWER ON THE STREETS

The Externals vs. the Internals—Fear vs. Personal Power

Traditional crime prevention and personal safety advice professes to educate citizens so that they do not become victims of crime. Government statistics scare the public. The often-quoted "Crime Clock" tells citizens that: One crime is committed every 2 seconds, one violent crime every 21 seconds, and one property crime every 3 seconds. These figures include one forcible rape every 6 minutes, one robbery every minute, and one motor vehicle theft every 24 seconds.[80] The media does its share in unnerving and frightening females. A newspaper headline reads: "1 in 8 U.S. women raped."[81] The article states that: "...five rapes out of six are not reflected in widely accepted crime statistics..."[82] One of my students who read this article told me that if she weren't taking the self-defense class for women she wouldn't know what to do—except wait or expect to be raped!

Women frequently are warned not to jog by themselves. Seniors are counseled not to go out after dark or to go to the bank in pairs, lest someone rob them of their social security checks. Young men often travel on their own. If a young woman expresses an interest in traveling by herself, she is threatened with being sold into the slave trade or at the least being raped. More general advice to women: make sure to have a male voice on your answering machine or don't walk across campus by yourself at night—call for a police escort. The message rings loud and clear: if you are a senior citizen, you cannot take care of yourself; if you are a woman, you cannot take care of yourself and you must be protected by a male. The problem with this type of "well-meaning" advice is that it all revolves around the presence of external factors—forces which are out of your control. I call them "the externals." "The externals " are used to scare you and leave you powerless. We cannot control forces outside of ourselves, but we can have control over ourselves, our choices, and our lives. These are "the internals"—our knowledge and the ability to take care of ourselves. We are in control and powerful. Personal safety can be approached from the position of personal choice, internal centering, and psychological strength.

"The externals"—the scare tactics—are totally out of line. These scare tactics are a means of social control—to frighten you into staying "in your place"—at the bottom of the glass pyramid and at the bottom of the heap. (See Chapter 7—Sexual Harassment.) The difference between "the externals"and "the internals" is that of *negative versus positive.* Negative advice is restrictive. It is council which is based on depressing, pessimistic, and bleak perspectives. The difference between "the externals" and "the internals" is also the difference between *don't's versus do's.* "Don't go out at night; don't walk by yourself; don't go on a trip by yourself." These "don't's" are restrictive, and sorely strain and restrict your sense of power and control. The scare tactics are designed to keep you in a box of fear. Our goal is freedom of choice and personal safety, without buying into the society's reactionary scare tactics. Internal control is based directly on your ability to take care of yourself—your capability to evaluate risks and to make choices based on your own decisions. This is how we keep our personal power in crime prevention.

Street Safety

Time: late at night
Location: a bad neighborhood in the city

Condition of streets: dark and deserted
Special circumstance: a rapist is on the prowl
Question: Who will he target?

Scenario One:

A woman is leaving work after a tiring day. She is preoccupied with events which transpired that day. She is having an important meeting the next day and is thinking about how best to handle it. She is on her way to her car, which is parked in a garage, five blocks away from her office. She is unaware of a noise behind her and continues on her way.

Scenario Two:

A second woman is leaving work. She is aware that she is walking through a bad neighborhood, that the streets are dark and deserted, and that her car is five blocks away. She is clearly apprehensive. She walks quickly, hoping that she will safely make it to her car. She hears a noise behind her, but is afraid to turn to look because, if she does, someone may actually be there.

Scenario Three:

A third woman leaves work. She, too, is aware that she is walking through a bad neighborhood, that the streets are dark and deserted, and that her car is five blocks away. Her body language indicates alertness and self-assurance. She hears a noise behind her and turns to look, thinking that if anyone tries to hurt her, he will be sorry he was ever born. She is psychologically and physically prepared.

Whom does the assailant target, and whom does he not approach? He probably would approach either of the first two women. The first woman was completely unaware. In practically every attack that has ever been reported to me that has occurred on the streets, the victim was not paying attention. To prove this, I would ask the person: "Where did the assailant come from?" The answer: "Nowhere," or "I don't know." The second woman made a good target because she was sending out body language that indicated that she was intimidated by the "externals"—the night, the dark, the deserted streets, the bad neighborhood, or the fear that a rapist might attack her. The third woman had internal power and control. She could not change the fact of who she was—a woman and, therefore, in a high-risk target group—and she could not change her location. What she did have control over was her attitude.

Street safety is important to all of us. We need to have the skills to go out on the streets with safety and self-confidence. We have the right to go where we choose to go, whenever we choose to go there, without having to be fearful for our personal safety.

The following are examples of traditional negative personal safety advice compared to positive personal power advice and solutions.

Jogging

Traditional Advice.

"Don't jog by yourself—it is not safe. If you must jog, make sure you jog with a friend." Women have been raped, kidnapped, or murdered going out on their own.

Effects.

Your schedule is restricted because you need to coordinate with someone else. The threat of physical assault elicits fear and makes the thought of jogging stressful.

Analysis and Impact.

Infrequent or inconvenient running schedule. Frequent aerobic exercise is essential for physical and psychological well-being. Loss of self-esteem and power because of implied inability to take care of yourself.

The Personal Power Solution.

If you cannot or do not choose to change "the externals," then change "the internals"—your attitude! Weigh your risks. A story comes to mind which is analogous to this cycle of fear that immobilizes women. In the early 1980's, people in the San Francisco Bay area were terrorized by the "Trailside Killer." This man raped and murdered a number of hikers on trails in the area. People were afraid to go hiking. A couple of male friends, whom my partner and I hiked with on a number of occasions, refused to go—they were frightened. We went on our own. The trail was practically deserted. I refused to fear that this man was going to jump out from behind the bushes. I was determined to enjoy my hike. What I did was heighten my level of awareness. I paid attention to what was going on around me and, in addition, carried a canister of C.S. tear gas (which I always have with me in any case). We enjoyed the hike, the scenery, and the fresh air. When the "Trailside Killer" was captured, the newspapers reported that he lived just three blocks from our friends!

Going Out Alone at Night

Traditional Advice.

If you don't have a man with you to protect you, then walk in a group.

Effects.

Your schedule is restricted. Loss of freedom. You may miss out on doing things or going places that are important to you.

Analysis and Impact.

You cannot take care of yourself; you are weak and vulnerable. If you need to be or choose to be out alone, fear may make you unsure of yourself.

The Personal Power Solution.

You can go out alone, day or night, if you choose to or need to. "Protection by a man" is no guarantee of your personal safety. The man may not even know how to fight, and you might end up having to protect him. Men get attacked also. A group is no guarantee of your personal safety either. Several years ago, a young woman reported to me that she was visiting Tiajuana, Mexico, with a group of her friends. It was getting dark, and they were on a footbridge, when she was separated from her friends by a gang of four men. The leader grabbed her from behind and tried to drag her off the bridge. Her friends did not know how to come to her defense and stood by, helpless. This young woman, who had taken my self-defense training, yelled at, and sprayed tear gas in the face of the leader of the group. She then sprayed another man. Within three seconds, these two men dropped down on the ground, screaming in pain. The young woman was so angry, she chased the other two men off the bridge. The only person you can depend on to defend you, or to take care of you, is you. You will feel wonderful and powerful when you realize you can defend yourself and win!

Street Smarts

To be safe on the streets you need to be not only a powerful person, in control of your own life, you also need to acquire skills and street smarts. How you dress, how you walk, what you carry with you, how you choose your routes are all factors that you need to take into consideration.

Clothing.

Traditional women's clothing puts women at a disadvantage on the streets. For many years, women's clothing has been made with few or no pockets, forcing a woman to carry a purse—thus occupying not only one arm and hand, but also, in addition, part of her concentration, since she knows that her purse is a vulnerable target. (A man's clothing, on the other hand, usually has many deep pockets, so that he is free to concentrate on the business at hand.) Dress codes often require that a woman wear high heels. Heels make it tricky to maintain your balance and stability and difficult, or impossible, to effectively run from danger. Fashion many times dictates skirts that are long or dresses that are tight—again, restricting freedom of movement. Combine a long, tight skirt, high heels, and a purse, and you have a potentially trapped prey for an assailant on the prowl.

Choose your clothing with both fashion and your personal safety in mind. Instead of a purse, you could wear a waist pack. If you do choose to carry a purse, I suggest that you keep it close to your body or under your coat—dangling purses are invitations to criminals. I would also suggest that you keep items in your purse to a minimum, so that you are not lugging a weighty, bulky burden. Many women wear sneakers to work and change into their "required" heels at the office. This excellent solution permits you to be appropriately dressed on the job and safer on the streets. I would also avoid dresses and skirts that prohibit movement. If you choose to wear restrictive clothing or footwear, then be aware of your increased vulnerability. To counter this vulnerability, practice physical fighting techniques dressed in heels and skirts.

Routes.

Be familiar with your routes. If you are going into an unfamiliar area, research it ahead of time. One reason many tourists are targeted for attack is that they look lost. Walk in a confident manner, as if you owned the street. If you must check a map, or directions, then do so in a safe area. If you pull out a map on the street, you have two strikes against you: one, you are indicating that you are unfamiliar with the area; and two, you are not aware of your surroundings.

Blend.

Try to blend in with the local population as much as possible. I would not wear anything, or do anything, that draws attention to myself.

Awareness.

You must always be alert on the streets. I am not saying that you must be tense or "on guard duty." What I am encouraging is for you to pay attention. Be alert, be aware, and know what is going on around you. Under normal, everyday circumstances, your body language indicates that you respect yourself, and that you are walking with self-confidence and assurance. Your strides are purposeful. Your radar is on, and you know what is going on around you—briefly glancing at people on the streets. If your intuition tells you that it is dangerous, then you need to magnify your level of awareness to the level which I call, "don't mess with me!" Your strides become even more purposeful. If you see people on the streets, you may look at them so that they know that you are aware of their presence. Your body language and your eyes clearly indicate "come near me, and you will be in big trouble!"

Street Hassling

Oftentimes, we are approached on the streets by someone asking for directions, for the time, or for some money. Your choice is to respond or not to respond. Be aware, however, that the individual's intent may be to test your vulnerability. A mugger may try to divert your attention. I have seen people search through their wallets or their purses to find money for people on the streets! This is a very unwise and dangerous practice. A rape attack is often preceded by verbal testing—to see if you can be intimidated. If you decide to respond to the query, then do so in a brief, businesslike manner. Do not allow yourself to be distracted. My best advice is to trust your intuition. If your gut feeling tells you that something is wrong, don't even respond to the other person. Walk by briskly, without acknowledging their request. (See Chapter 5—Acquaintance Rape Avoidance and Defense.)

Additional Skills.

A knowledge of physical self-defense skills is invaluable. Physical self-defense is a back-up to psychological and preventative skills. You enhance your ability to prevent an attack if you know that you can successfully incapacitate an assailant (See Chapter 9—Physical Self-Defense.)

Fighting Street Harassment

Street harassment consists of unsolicited comments of a sexual nature and physical violations such as grabbing and pinching (See Chapter 7—Sexual Harassment.) Street harassment is on the same continuum as rape and sexual harassment. It is so pervasive that I believe that the "Crime Clock", quoted earlier in this chapter, would blow up and fly off the wall if it tried to keep a tally. Women are its victims—they are not to be blamed.

Street harassment is another assault on women's self-esteem and self-respect. Not only does it assail women's dignity, but it violates privacy and the right to be left alone in public. It turns the streets into a battle-zone in which the threat alone is enough to cause stress and anxiety.

Why do males consider it their right, privilege, and duty to intrude? Why is it so steeped into the male psyche? Some men do it as a form of "backlash"[83] —to keep feminists in "their place"—by objectifying women. They also do it to threaten women—reminding women that males are predators and that women are subjected to rape. Other males use street harassment as a form of male bonding or as a right of passage—passed on from father to son. Some very misguided men think that women actually like it. Some very misguided women think that it is a compliment and are flattered by a man's whistle—not realizing that the same man would whistle at a sack of potatoes if the sack had a female symbol on it.

Strategies

Just as in rape, men often try to blame the victim. This is a form of social control: dictating what a women should and shouldn't wear, how she should walk, and what areas she should avoid—so that she could prevent harassment. Your response to street harassment depends on several factors: your analysis of the situation, your perception of danger, and your own choices.

Daytime, Commonplace Non -Physical , Verbal Harassment.

The goal of the male is to frazzle you. To achieve his aim, he needs to irk you and provoke you into a response. If he is with others, he may loose face if he does not succeed. If the situation appears to be physically non-threatening, your response depends upon your disposition at the time. If you don't want to be bothered to take any of your valuable time and energy dealing with a "sub-humanoid," then purposefully disregard his presence. To intentionally disregard his presence, continue your normal stride, while keeping a poker face. (Watch him from the corner of your eye to make sure that the situation has not escalated.) When you don't respond to his volley of insults, the ball is back on his court and he, in turn, becomes upset. You know you have won this skirmish when the pitch of his voice is higher and the yell is louder. Your benefit from this type of non-response is that you stay calm and centered, and are able to continue on your way without the disruption of a fight or flight adrenalin rush.

Suppose you are walking down the street, and a man says "Good morning" to you. Do you ignore him or answer him? Again, this depends on your disposition and upon your perception of his intent. If you consider his statement entirely innocent, and you choose to respond, then do so. If you do not choose to answer him, you don't have to—ignore him and go about your business. If you have ignored him and he counters "What's the matter with you, stuck up or something?", your assessment of his harassment was correct and your behavior completely appropriate.

Sometimes you may elect to confront the individual who is attempting to challenge you. For example, you have had an extremely frustrating day and your comfort zone is nonexistent. Your temper is barely in check when some hapless man starts to confront you with lewd animalistic sounds. You can use this opportunity to vent your anger and frustration at him. Yell at him to crawl back under his rock or insult his manhood. If others are around, I suggest a loud nasty public scene, where all the attention of the passersby would be focused on him. Words such as "filthy pervert" would be appropriate. Make sure that you make eye contact and that your body language as well as your verbal language reflect your anger.

Daytime or Public Physical Harassment.

The goal of the deviate is to take you by surprise—pinching you on the buttocks or grabbing your breast(s). If this is done on the streets, he tries to make a quick get-away. If he is in close quarters with you, such as on a crowded elevator or on public transportation, he attacks quickly and then tries to blend into the crowd. You prevent this from happening by being aware of your surroundings and by sensing what is going on around you. If you catch him in the act, forcefully slam him off of you (a karate block works wonders). Then yell at the top of your lungs: "Get your hands off of me, you filthy pervert! What would your wife (or mother) say if she knew you were doing this?" He will be embarrassed. If he tries to say anything in his own defense, you can yell at him that you intend to have him arrested—physical harassment, being a form of sexual battery and assault is illegal.[84] If you do contact the police and do want to file charges, insist that the police officer take the report. Police have not had a good history of cooperation in these matters.[85] If the officer is uncooperative and you wish to pursue the matter, then contact his supervisor or the officer in charge of the police station.

Street Harassment in Dangerous Circumstances.

If you are fairly isolated, if it is nighttime, or if you are in a dangerous area, you may choose to respond differently than in the public, daytime street harassment situations described above. Verbal harassment in an unsafe area is not street harassment. I consider it a threat from a potential assailant. Your appropriate behavior in this instance would be to send out "don't mess with me" signals which convince the assailant, in no uncertain terms, to leave you alone. If he approaches, you may have to utilize a combination of physical and psychological techniques to fight him off. If the harassment is physical, rather than verbal, it is a physical assault and I would respond appropriately, utilizing psychological and, if necessary, physical defense techniques to attack him.

Car Safety and Carjacking Prevention

Times were when we felt safe in our cars. Newspaper and media reports of carjackings have made citizens angry and frightened. A spokesman for the American Automobile Association told the Associated Press: "People are accosted at traffic lights, when they're pumping gas, when they're bumped and pull over. Some of these incidents have occurred in broad daylight, during the normal rush hour."[86] The problem has become so pervasive that the AAA is compiling reports of road violence, and the Federal Bureau of Alcohol, Tobacco and Firearms has set up a hotline for victims of armed carjackings. [87]

Another personal space has been invaded! If we can't even drive our cars (because it is not safe), or use mass transportation (because, in many cases, it is even less safe), or walk (which may in some cases be even less safe than taking mass transportation), then what are we supposed to do? Stay confined to our homes? Become prisoners of our fear?

The principles of personal power apply in this situation as well as in any other. As I mentioned earlier in this chapter, in practically every attack that has ever been reported to me that has occurred on the streets, the victim was not paying attention. In order for you to be safe in your car, you also need to be aware.

Before Entering Your Car

Have your key ready before you enter your car. Many people get attacked at their car doors because they are searching for the correct key and are not paying attention. Be alert as you approach your car. Look into the back seat area before you unlock and open the door. Use a miniature high-intensity flashlight if it is dark—these inexpensive lights can be purchased in most hardware or home improvement stores. Many can be attached to a key ring or clipped to your pocket or purse. If someone pops up from behind the driver's seat as you are driving along, and points a gun to your head or knife to your throat, it is too late to do anything about it. However, you can prevent this from happening 100%! As soon as you are safely in your car, lock your doors and keep your windows closed.

Upon Entering Your Car

Immediately lock your doors and keep your windows closed. Leave nothing on the seats or in view that would attract attention—such as a purse or other valuables.

General Tips

Keep your gas key separate from any other keys, and make sure your address is not to be found anywhere in the car. If you normally keep your registration in the glove compartment, I would suggest that you photocopy the registration, carry the duplicate on you, and keep the original wherever you keep your important documents. If you need to leave anything in the car, lock it in the trunk before you reach your final destination.

While Driving

Evaluate the situation. You are in control; therefore, you determine when you consider the situation dangerous and wish to take extra precautions. If you consider the situation potentially dangerous, then expand your internal radar—your level of awareness. Keep the radio volume down, so that you can hear what is going on around you. When you stop at a traffic light or stop sign, be extremely alert and keep your car in gear—in first or in drive. That way, if someone who looks suspicious comes near your car, you can take off immediately! You can do a couple of things to avoid being trapped or boxed-in. One is, when you stop, allow enough distance between you and the car ahead of you so that you can maneuver your car. A second is, when there are two lanes of traffic, drive in the outside lane. This strategy, too, will allow you to turn your car and move out of harm's way. If your car is surrounded , blast your horn and drive off—don't go zero to sixty in 15 seconds, but fast enough to move out of danger. Just as on the streets, be extremely alert to trickery. Criminals have been known to bump your car from behind. When you get out to check for damage, they attack. If your instinct tells you that something is wrong, don't get out of the car. Just take off! Do not stop to pick up hitchhikers. If you see someone in need of assistance and wish to help, go to the nearest phone and dial 911. This way you will avoid danger and, at the same time, you can call for qualified assistance to help the person. If someone is following you, drive to the nearest police station, fire station, hospital emergency room, or as a last resort, an attended 24-hour gas station. As soon as you arrive, start blasting your horn to attract attention.

Parking and Getting Out of Your Car.

In an urban area, try to park in a well-trafficked area rather than on a quiet side street. At nighttime, or if it will be dark when you return to your car, park under a light. In certain parts of a city, you may wish to park in a parking lot or garage. Make sure that the parking lot or garage is well-lit , is attended, and will be attended when you return to your car. Park as close to the attendant as you can. Look before you get out. If you don't feel comfortable, then don't park there. Go elsewhere.

Car safety need not be a burden. Driving is a way of life and a necessity for many of us. By developing a personal safety consciousness, you reduce your risks and maintain control of your environment.

Keeping Your Personal Power

Your personal safety is in your own hands. You are completely in charge of yourself and of your own well-being. You cannot depend on the police to protect you, nor on the good graces of a stranger who happens to be passing by, nor on your husband or boyfriend or anyone else. You must depend on yourself. When you count on yourself, you acknowledge your internal strengths, abilities, and prowess. You are in control and do not permit external forces and fears to daunt you. You are freed from your box of fear and can go forward to direct your own life.

NINE

PHYSICAL SELF-DEFENSE
"It Is Not The Size Of The Cat In The Fight..."

PHYSICAL SELF-DEFENSE
"It Is Not The Size Of The Cat In The Fight..."

Why Women Need to Learn How to Fight

If, as I firmly believe, self-defense is at least 75 percent psychological, and I place major emphasis in this area, then why do women still need to learn how to fight? Why couldn't a woman mainly rely on preventive and psychological techniques to keep an assailant away? You can keep assailants away for the most part by utilizing preventive and psychological techniques; however, physical self-defense is really that important. You need to be able to back up the prevention and psychological skills. By having the knowledge and ability to take care of yourself physically, you will actually reduce the chance of having to use the physical defense skills. Knowing that you can fight back effectively and win enhances your psychological arsenal—you will walk a little taller and with a lot more confidence.

It is Not the Size of the Cat in the Fight ...

Over the years I have learned a tremendous amount about the psychology of physical defense and the physical aspects of self-defense from my cats. Cats, compared to humans, are relatively small creatures. Yet, as cat owners would agree, they are an amazing, almost larger than life, presence.

Peter

Peter was my first very own cat. He came to live with me when I was in the Army and stationed in Texas. When Peter was 9 months old, I returned to New York to visit my parents. My parents had a back yard which seemed to be inhabited by many neighborhood cats. Shortly after my arrival, I happened to look out the back window and couldn't believe what I saw: ten to fifteen cats climbing the back wall and scattering in every direction. I heard a loud, deep, growling sound. I went outside and saw an animal whom I did not recognize: a huge cat, standing alone in the center of the yard, three times Peter's size, with an enormous tail. I looked again. The cat looked more or less Siamese—Peter's breed. But then, Peter was still a kitten. I called out "Peter?" It was Peter. He had chased all the neighborhood cats out of his yard! He didn't take the number of his opponents, or their size, into consideration. Peter had created a force field of fury and cleared the yard!

Tascha

T. Tascha Tootchkins The Terrible Terror was aptly named. Tascha was known for biting everybody—she was indiscriminate. If you looked the wrong way at her or displeased her in anyway, she would bite you. Yet, one night Tascha became a heroine. Several intruders tried to enter my home. I could hear them at the front door, trying to break in. My German Shepherd dog, Heather, who was a puppy at the time, was useless. She didn't even know how to bark! Peter ran under the bed. I dialed the local Department of Public Safety, told them that there was a break-in in progress and gave them the address. Before the police could ever respond to my call, Tascha transformed into a mountain lion! She ran to the front door and growled and snarled and roared at the would-be intruders. She created such a commotion, that they, fearful for their lives and not knowing what kind of animal was at the door, left. I learned from Tascha about the effectiveness of the sound of fury.

Bast

I was hosting a Labor Day barbecue. People were out on the deck, grilling their hot dogs and hamburgers, chatting, and having a good time. One guest had brought her dog, Amber, a seventy pound retriever. My German Shepherd, Heather, was visiting with the other dog. All of a sudden, a fight broke out. The dogs went at each other with a fury. Fur was flying and the dogs were growling and snarling at each other. My guests were very upset, and did not know what to do. Amber had Heather pinned down when, all of a sudden, Bast, my six pound Burmese cat, came on the scene. She ran across the back yard; jumped onto the deck; and spread-eagle and screaming, leaped at both dogs' heads, attacking and bloodying Amber's nose. She gave the appearance of an eagle descending on its prey! The fight was broken up and Heather hung around the deck, accepting hot dogs from sympathetic people. Bast and Amber were nowhere to be found. An hour later I located them. Bast had Amber cornered under the deck. Amber was cowering; Bast's body language indicated: "Don't you move or you will be sorry!" How could one six pound cat intimidate a seventy pound dog? Simply put, it is not the size of the cat in the fight, it is the size of the fight in the cat!

Hershey

At the age of thirteen, Bast's sister, Hershey became my heroine. Tigre du Lys, our outside, half-wild, adopted cat, needed her annual shots. The only way to catch Tigre was to grab her when she came inside for a meal. The idea was for my partner to hold the carrying case and for me to place the cat inside. I picked Tigre up and she screamed "bloody murder!" I knew that if I let go of this cat, she would be impossible to catch. I yelled to my partner to hurry up and bring over the case. The tone and pitch of my voice was distressful—I was holding a furious-sounding, angry, unpredictable animal. Hershey, a small Burmese, came to my defense. She ran over and repeatedly jumped over four feet in the air to attack Tigre, swatting at her head. It didn't matter that Tiger was twice her size, or much younger. Hershey, with no doubts, or second thoughts in her mind, attacked. Hershey had the courage and determination to win, no matter what!

Jasmine

A friend of mine, Pame, told me the story of how Jasmine, a small Manx was able to stand her ground against a much larger cat. "I found out that Jasmine's favorite pal was named Gordo... . He was roughly three times her weight and size. ...he would come over every morning to visit... . These two kittens loved to wrestle...but with Gordo being so much bigger he had a distinct advantage. However, Jasmine never seemed to let him get the better of her. For the longest time it puzzled me how she managed to get the best of him. I discovered her secret one day during a particularly loud wrestling match. I walked outside to try to break up the skirmish. Jasmine had just managed to wriggle free of Gordo's grasp. What happened next surprised me. Jasmine stood her ground, [and] flattened her ears back against her head... . Gordo circled around her trying to discover a weak spot. Jasmine countered every move and kept her defense up. Then suddenly she did something unexpected: she attacked. She went straight for his testicles and in no time all you could see of Gordo was his rear end, as he high tailed it for home."[88] So, Jasmine teaches us to go for vulnerable areas.

Sir Maxwell

Max is a very handsome, sable Burmese. He is the epitome of the laid-back Californian. So one day, when I saw Sir Max roll over on his side with his feet curled up in the air, I thought that he was being cute. Max's sister, Lady Blue, came over to check things out and Maxwell attacked! It turned out that he was in fighting position. Normally, I don't advocate that you fight from the ground. This is because you do not have the agility of a cat, and, unlike a cat, you cannot easily roll over and run off on all fours. But, if you are thrown down, or caught in a lying down position, you, too, are in excellent fighting position.

Since your legs are longer and stronger than your opponent's arms, you can kick to incapacitate—either break a knee cap or kick the groin.

The Laws of Self-Defense

The laws of self-defense in California (which are representative of most state laws) state that it is lawful to defend oneself if one is being physically attacked, or if, as a reasonable person, one believes that bodily injury is about to be inflicted. You may use whatever force is reasonable or necessary under the circumstances to prevent injury to yourself. You can meet force with force, but the force must not be excessive to the perceived danger. For example, in the story in Chapter 2, my partner was threatened by a man who came up very close and menaced her with a pipe wrench. It would have been considered self-defense for her to have broken the man's kneecap. It would not have been self-defense if she had continued to attack him, because he would have already been incapacitated. Remember, also, that self-defense must be immediate. It is not self-defense to attack someone after the danger has passed.

How to Fight Effectively

Physical self-defense encompasses the knowledge and practical application of physical defense skills. For a complete, detailed guide to learning physical fighting skills, I highly recommend my book, Are You A Target? A Guide To Self-Protection and Personal Safety. Are You A Target? (Torrance Publishing Company), will provide you with a comprehensive approach to learning physical defense techniques. The book is easy to understand and apply, and contains 86 "how-to" photographs. I also suggest that you consider enrolling in a good self-defense class.

Women's Self-Defense is Not Martial Arts

You do not need to be a black belt in karate to learn how to fight effectively and win. One reason why many women don't even attempt to learn self-defense skills is that they think that it takes years of training. A woman may choose to take up a form of martial arts as a discipline. Good for her—she will accrue many benefits. However, many women don't have the time or inclination to study a martial art. The myth persists that a short-term self-defense class will not teach her to fight effectively. This couldn't be further from the truth. Once you become attuned to the psychology of self-defense (See Chapter 2—The Psychology of Empowerment), the physical skills are not difficult to learn.

The main similarity between self-defense for women and martial arts is that both employ physical fighting skills. Modern karate is a sport as well as a martial art. "The point system of the karate free-fighting matches was devised specifically with the limitations of striking areas in order to measure the skill and ability of body movements."[89] Modern karate encompasses physical fitness and the discipline of both mind and body—"Mental discipline, self-confidence, and self-control... ."[90] Self-defense is not a sport. When I developed self-defense skills from karate skills, I eliminated the sporting aspects. For example, instead of kicking at an area, such as the kneecap, you kick through the target.

Physical Defense Skills Must be Simple

In order to learn and remember physical defense skills, they must be simple. Fancy-looking, flashy techniques are O.K. for Hollywood, but they have no place in women's self-defense. One of the main criteria I use to judge the effectiveness of a skill used to teach women is "can it be remembered in one year or even in five or ten years?"

Target Accessible Vulnerable Body Areas

If you look at a chart of vulnerable targets in the human body, you might be surprised that there are so many of them. One source lists twenty-eight vital spots![91] When women who have not yet learned self-defense attempt to attack an assailant physically, they will, for the most part, aim at a non-vulnerable area (such as the shin) or an area that men automatically know how to protect (the groin.) Consistently hitting non-vulnerable areas is a "non-skill." The reason for this ineffective attack is the social conditioning that women have received (See Chapter 2—The Psychology of Empowerment).

You attack vulnerable body areas to incapacitate an assailant quickly. Vulnerable areas of the body cannot be strengthened by body building or physical exercise. In many cases, stopping an assailant by striking one of these areas does not take a lot of strength, force, or power.

The principle of targeting is simple: you attack whatever vulnerable area you can get to, with whatever you have to attack it, and with as much force as you have available. And, as I stated above, strike through the area, rather than at it.

Target areas.

I recommend attacking the following areas: the eyes, the temples, the base of the nose, the Adam's apple, the windpipe, the groin (but only if it is a surprise), the kneecap, and the side of the kneecap. In success stories, reported to me, the areas hit most frequently have been the eyes (tear gas), the kneecap (kick), and Adam's apple (punch).

Weapons.

Use whatever you have available to attack those target areas: your fists (punching), your feet (kicking), your elbows, your fingers or thumbs (for the eyes). I highly recommend C.S.

tear gas and stun guns which I will discuss later in this chapter. Remember, the use of any of these weapons, including your own fists or feet, requires training and practice.

Best Attacks

The following are the three best attacks that have been reported to me in success stories over the years: (1) break the knee cap, (2) punch the Adam's apple, and (3) spray the assailant in the face with tear gas. Take the stance as you are attacking.

Take the Stance.

Get into your stance by first turning your side to the assailant. Place your legs a comfortable distance apart. Bend your knees, keeping your torso erect, and your body balanced on the balls of both feet, so that you are evenly crouching or "sitting" into the stance. Bend your arms at the elbows, holding them a little away from your body. Make a clenched fist (described below). Look directly into the assailant's eyes with an intimidating "don't mess with me!" glare.

Smash the Adam's Apple.

Clench your fists so that your wrist is tight, your fingers are curled into your palm, and your thumbs are curled on the outside of your fingers. As you punch, your wrist is turned down. You make contact with the flat part of the fist. Put your body weight into the move and hit as hard as you can, punching through the Adam's apple.

Break the Knee Cap.

One skill that I teach which my students will not forget how to do is to kick through the kneecap. This is one of the best ways of incapacitating an assailant, is easy to do, is easy to remember, and is hard to defend against. To do this, bring your knee up so that your thigh is parallel to the ground; flex your ankle so that your toes are pointing upward; and kick with all your force, using a pendulum swing, to bring the ball of your foot through the assailant's knee cap.

Spray the Assailant in the Face with Tear Gas.

It takes less than 3 seconds to blind an assailant temporarily with tear gas. Aim at his face, viciously yell, and spray. Continue spraying until he stops his attack.

Grabs

If someone grabs your wrist or arm, immediately break free. The most vulnerable area of the grasp is the upper part of the thumb joint. Immediately yell and, at the same time, forcefully twist into his thumb joint. If you cannot break out, kick his knee cap. If circumstances warrant it, you may want to break the kneecap before you break out of a hold.

If you are grabbed from the rear, forcefully stomp down on the instep of the attacker's foot (you will be able to feel him close to you); pivot toward him; and, with your inside forearm, whack him in the Adam's apple.

Practice, Practice, Practice

Even though I advocate simple physical skills, in order to be effective they must be integrated into your total being in such a way that they are performed automatically and without hesitation. Ever see a champion tennis player serve a ball, or a professional golfer drive a ball? Their delivery seems so easy that it looks natural. Try to serve an ace or sink a hole-in-one without practice. It is very difficult to do. The archery coach at Brooklyn College of the City University of New York was amazed that I won every tournament. Her archers would sweat for hours trying to hit the gold consistently. Sure I went to practice. I went through my practice rounds and left. They couldn't understand. My secret? I had been shooting since before the age of ten and had, through consistent practice, become so good at it that archery was second nature to me. I didn't even have to think. The arrows flew right into the gold!

Your kicking, punching, blocking, and whatever physical skills you learn for self-defense must be so good that they become second nature. In a crisis situation, you cannot take the time to think about how to take your stance or where to place your feet or how to make a fist.

When you practice physical skills, sometimes you may want to practice with a partner. Your selection is extremely important. Your partner can be a man or woman. It doesn't matter. Do not practice with someone who has an ego problem—who laughs at you or who tries to show you how skilled he is at your expense or discourages you by telling you that you can't effectively fight back. Remember, this is practice. Your partner wouldn't want you to actually incapacitate him. This type of person is only preparing you to loose. Only choose to practice with someone who encourages you and helps you. You need positive reinforcement.

Use Your Voice as a Weapon

One of the most difficult tasks I have encountered in teaching women to fight is how to utilize one of the most important psychological and physical defense weapons that they have: their voice. A physical defense or attack cannot be effectively executed without yelling. In Chapter 4, we discussed how research studies found yelling to be one of the most important resistance strategies. In order to fight back effectively and win, you must yell! Reach deep into your inner self, breathe from your diaphragm, and belt out a loud, blood curdling battle cry! This battle cry enhances your force field of fury and many times is enough to propel the assailant away from you.

Be Prepared to Act Immediately

Upon attack or threat of attack (or if you consider the situation dangerous), be prepared to act automatically. Breathe deeply. Keep your mind flexible and fluid. If the assailant attacks you or is about to attack you, attack first.

Combine Psychological with Physical Skills

Physical attacks are enormously more effective if you combine them with psychological skills. The more ways that you can convince an assailant that he has chosen the wrong person, the better. Remember that your mind and body are interrelated. Suppose, for example, you are waiting for a bus. A stranger approaches and starts to threaten you. If you quietly say, "leave me alone," he probably won't. So how do you quickly convince him to leave? You combine body language, verbal language, and eye contact. You get into your stance, look directly into his eyes with a piercing glare, and leaning or moving toward him, yell at him to get away from you. In effect, you have created a very loud force field of fury. He will leave. If he doesn't leave and tries to attack you, attack him!

Best Strategies

As discussed in Chapter 4, your best fighting strategies are a combination of three skills: yelling, physical resistance, and running away. Active resistance is the key to successful self-defense.

Women and Guns

The decision of whether to purchase a gun for self-defense is one of personal choice. What I would like to do in this section is to provide you with information so that you can make a decision that works for you.

The Growth of Female Handgun Ownership

The female gun market has grown dramatically in recent years—with over twelve million women owning handguns, and more than 17 percent of U.S. pistol owners being women, up from 10 percent in 1984. A Gallup poll commissioned by Smith & Wesson found 15 million more women who were interested in buying guns.[92]

Why has there been such an extraordinary increase in gun ownership among women? Three reasons come to mind: (1) the increase in our society of violence in general and toward women in particular; (2) the growth in the number of women living alone and of single women raising children; and (3) the targeting of women for sales by gun manufacturers, coupled with an aggressive advertising campaign. The first two factors have contributed to a perception of increased vulnerability on the part of many women and an increased recognition by these women of the need to protect themselves. Yet, if you take a close look at government statistics, the National Crime Survey (NCS) shows uneven trends in violent crime. "NCS data on rape, robbery, and aggravated and simple assault show that these crimes increased from 1973 to 1981, dropped between 1981 and 1986, and have increased slightly since then. Nevertheless, 1989 levels were 11% below the peak year of 1981."[93] Since 1985, the Uniform Crime Report index of criminal incidents reported to law enforcement agencies has evidenced increases in all categories of violent crime.[94] What has changed dramatically is the target marketing of women by the handgun industry.

Why Women Are the New Target of the Handgun Industry

In 1975, domestic handgun production, rounded to the nearest 100,000 was 1.8 million. Domestic handgun production increased every year until it peaked in 1982 with 2.6 million handguns being produced.[95] Then, production declined steadily every year until 1986 when 1.5 million handguns were produced.

Apparently, the market was saturated. In fact, Smith & Wesson conducted a study and found that 29 percent of men were interested in owning a gun, but 28 percent already had one.[96] "The gun industry found its savior, and she was middle-aged, middle-to upper income, professional, and of varying political stripes. She was on her own in the 1980's, taking advantage of the gains accrued by the women's rights movement. Liberation, however, couldn't wipe out a sense of vulnerability propelled by violence against women. Well-published reports of alarming statistics—such as the FBI estimate that a woman in the United States is raped every six minutes—fueled the fear.[97] In 1989, Smith &Wesson launched a full-blown national advertising campaign aimed at women. The ads played on the emotions. The fear-based advertisements purported to offer safety tips, yet increased women's levels of anxiety. One ad pictures a woman lying in bed with a frightened look on her face. The caption reads, "Things that go 'bump' in the night aren't always your imagination."[98] It says to call the police and stay calm. "It's true you may have imagined the whole thing. But then again you may not."[99] This ad did not feature a gun, but pictured the Smith & Wesson logo and toll-free number for information about personal safety (and its LadySmith gun line).

A few months before this national ad campaign, in late 1988, Smith & Wesson released a line of pistols called the "LadySmith." The ads for the LadySmith series are compellingly seductive, with the handguns being promoted as sleek, frosted-blue .38 caliber pistols with slim grips designed for small hands. The San Francisco Chronicle found the "LadySmith" advertisements written in a "script so feminine it looks like an invitation to tea." [100]

Some national magazines, such as Good Housekeeping, Woman's Day, Mademoiselle, Glamour, Self, and Better Homes and Gardens refused to run the advertisements. Molly Yard, the NOW president at the time, denounced the campaign as an effort to "hoodwink women."[101] "Ms. and Glamour editorialized against Smith & Wesson's advertising campaign, arguing that women should not be lulled into a false sense of security by purchasing a gun and that any panic-motivated purchase could lead more readily to gun-related accidents. Wrote Ms. Magazine: Smith & Wesson makes us ask 'Who's preying on whom?' "[102]

The advertising campaign created quite a stir in the national media.It was so successful that Smith & Wesson put subsequent models on the market. According to Chris Dolnack, Smith & Wesson's public relations manager, Smith & Wesson was gearing up for a new ad campaign (aimed at professional women, ages 25 - 49) in which the handgun would be part of a personal security plan.[103]

Guns and Self-Defense

Are guns practical, useful tools in self-defense? The National Rifle Association (NRA) and the U.S. Department of Justice differ in opinions. The NRA likes to cite a 1979 Department of Justice study that shows that out of 32,000 attempted rapes, only 3 percent of attempts against armed individuals were successful. [104] This figure is misleading according to Michael Rand, a statistician with the Justice Department, because it is based only on 600 armed women out of the 32,000 rape attempts. [105] Moreover, the Department of Justice reports that "in only one half of 1 percent of all intended or actual instances of violent crime was a firearm even available to the victim."[106]

The Availability of Handguns for Self-Defense

Although each state regulates the availability of firearms, in most states it is illegal for citizens to carry a loaded handgun on one's person, or in a vehicle, while in urban and suburban areas. Handguns, though, can very easily be purchased since very few restrictions apply. In some states, an individual can walk into a gun store and purchase a handgun over the counter.

In California, for example, a resident over 21 who is not a convicted felon and who is not addicted to narcotics and who has not had a history of documented psychological problems may own a firearm. There is a fifteen day waiting period and a background check is made before legal transfer can be made. It is legal to own, possess, and keep a loaded handgun in one's place of residence or place of business. Therefore, in most cases, a handgun would be purchased for self-protection in the home.

The Dangers of Having a Gun in the Home

One of the factors which must be considered in the decision as to whether or not to purchase a gun is whether the benefits outweigh the hazards. Let us look at some statistics. The New England Journal of Medicine published an analysis of firearm-related deaths in the home. They found that a gun in the home is 43 times more likely to kill a family member or acquaintance in an accident or suicide than it is to kill an intruder.[107] The Center to Prevent Handgun Violence compiled the following facts about children and handguns:

- "Gunshot wounds to children ages 16 and under have tripled in major urban areas since 1986.
- "Firearm murders of youngsters 19 and under increased 125 percent between 1984 and 1990.
- "More than 1.2 million elementary-aged, latch-key children have access to guns in their homes.
- "In 1990, gun accidents were the fifth-leading cause of accidental death for children ages 14 and under.
- "A study of 266 accidental shootings of children ages 16 and under revealed that 50 percent of accidents occurred in the victims' homes, and 38 percent occurred in the homes of friends or relatives. The handguns used were most often (45%) found in bedrooms. Boys were predominantly the victims (80%) and shooters (92%).
- "The suicide rate of adolescents has tripled in the past three decades, making suicide the third-leading killer of teen-

agers. Guns are the leading method used by teenagers to commit suicide (60%), and nine out of ten attempted suicides involving handguns are completed." [108]

- "Most teen suicides are impulsive, with little or no planning, and 70 percent occur in the victim's homes.
- "A suicidal teenager living in a home with an easily-accessible gun is more likely to commit suicide than a suicidal teenager living in a home where no gun is present." [109]

A Personal Decision

When I was in the military, I earned sharpshooter medals for both rifle and pistol and was the only woman member of the 5th U.S. Army Pistol Team. Once, on the practice range, I learned the meaning of gun safety first hand. After firing some rounds, I placed my automatic (pistol) face down on the table, with the barrel facing the shooting range. This was a standard safety procedure. Good thing I did because the gun discharged on its own.

On one occasion I had to utilize my target pistols for self-defense. I was living alone in an apartment complex in San Antonio, Texas. A sergeant, who lived in the same complex and worked on the same army post as I did, came to my door drunk one evening. He wanted to have a relationship with me, and I wasn't interested. He banged on my door and threatened to harm me if I did not let him in. He was very loud, abusive, and violent. I took both my pistols out of their cases, loaded them, and pointed them in the direction of the door. I yelled: "If you don't get out of here, I am going to shoot you! I have two loaded pistols in my hands!" He left.

The decision as to whether to purchase a firearm is up to you. It is a personal choice. I would definitely caution against keeping a handgun in the home if : (1) there are children in the home, (2) a member of the household has a tendency toward depression, or (3) anyone in the household has a bad temper. My choice would be to go with the statistics. No matter how much of an equalizer a gun is and no matter how powerful it may make you feel, under the circumstances mentioned above, the numbers overwhelmingly indicate that the dangers of having a gun in the home outweigh the benefits. If none of these factors exists, then you need to do some very serious thinking. Are you willing to possibly kill someone? What if you shoot an intruder and don't kill him? What if the "intruder" is actually a family member coming home unexpectedly? Are you willing to take the chance of making a fatal mistake? If you are threatened with physical attack, would you be able to shoot an assailant without hesitation? Are you willing to do what it takes to become proficient with a weapon. Are you willing to keep up a practice schedule so that your skills with a handgun become second nature? If your answers to these questions are "Yes," then you may wish to consider a gun as part of your self-defense program. If you do choose to purchase a gun, it is important to do a lot of research before you make your purchase. Find out the differences between different types and calibers of various handguns. Purchase the best quality gun that fits your budget. You also may want to consider a rifle or shotgun. Check with your local police department and/or the National Rifle Association (NRA) about local gun laws, safety, and training. Be sure to take a firearms safety course which has been approved by the NRA and to keep up your practice on a regular basis on the range.

Non-Lethal Self-Defense Weapons—Tear Gas and Stun Guns

Even if you choose a handgun for home protection, you may not be legally able to carry your weapon on the streets. (See section titled The Availability of Handguns for Self-Defense in this chapter). I personally carry tear gas with me when I leave my home or office. My business partner carries a stun gun. Both are non-lethal weapons, and both are extremely effective in incapacitating assailants for approximately fifteen minutes. You are causing no permanent damage to the assailant, yet you are giving yourself a chance to get away safely.

One of the most frequent arguments against carrying tear gas or a stun gun is the threat or fear that it may be taken away and used against its owner. This does not happen if the person carrying it is aware and is familiar and comfortable with its use. I do not believe in carrying a weapon unless I know how to use it and I have practiced using it properly. In twelve years of conducting tear gas certification classes in California, only one individual has reported to me that her tear gas was taken away from her. The woman was so angry that she chased the aggressor down the street and retrieved her canister.

Another reason that I favor tear gas and stun guns is that they are non-lethal. You do not even have to think about, let alone answer, the question that you must ask yourself if you wish to use a gun for self-defense: "Are you willing to kill someone?"

Tear gas and stun guns, when carried and used properly, can give you an extra measure of protection. More knowledge about self-defense and non-lethal self-defense weapons can only increase your ability to take care of yourself and reduce your risk of being assaulted.

Tear Gas and O.C.

Tear gas is an irritant which, when shot into the face, causes temporary blindness, tearing, pain, and a stinging and burning sensation. It also causes coughing and sneezing and difficulty in breathing. The individual may panic and experience a period of dizziness and disorientation. It takes under three seconds to incapacitate an assailant by temporarily blinding him, and if you give him a good blast of the irritant, the effects should last for fifteen to thirty minutes. You can stop an assailant who is close to you or who is ten to fifteen feet away (depending on the canister,) and you can also stop multiple assailants. Tear gas is a very benign weapon. Since you are causing no permanent damage, there is no moral question or psychological hesitation on the part of the person defending herself. Since state laws vary, check with your local law enforcement agency on the legalities of the possession and use of tear gas for self-defense in your state.

Three types of chemical defense sprays are on the market C.N.(chloroacetophenone), C.S (othochlorobenzlmalononitrile), and O.C. (oleoresin capsicum.) C.N. (which is commonly known as "mace") is the weakest form of tear gas and may not work if the assailant is drunk, is under the influence of drugs, is experiencing certain forms of mental illness, or is hysterical. This is because it works on the nerve centers of the body which control pain. If those nerve centers are depressed, it may not work. C.S. is the type of tear gas used by the military. It is a stronger, longer lasting, and more punishing chemical agent than C.N. Since C.S. is stronger, it works on most assailants. Both chemicals react in two and a half to three seconds in the open eye—causing the eyes to close involuntarily, causing temporary blindness. C.S. also has a greater effect on the respiratory system then C.N. Tear gas causes a stinging and burning sensation on the skin. C.N. affects the skin more rapidly than C.S. This is of little consequence since you do not incapacitate an assailant by causing a stinging or burning sensation on his skin—you incapacitate an assailant by temporarily blinding him. I personally prefer C.S. tear gas. My primary reason for this is that C.S. is more effective on rapists since many rapists are intoxicated when they attack.

O.C. (pepper spray), is an oleoresin capsicum derivative and is a newer form of chemical spray. The main difference between C.N./C.S. tear gas, and O.C., is that the former are irritants, while the latter is an inflamatory agent. Depending on its concentration, (2 to 10%), O.C. can be a powerful inflammatory agent. It causes swelling of the eyes and airways, causing limited vision and difficulty in breathing. It also causes a burning sensation on the skin. [110] If you are interested using any of these products, check your state laws.

Stun Guns

Stun guns are non-lethal, "space-age," electronic weapons. In fact, the advanced circuitry converts the power of a nine volt bolt battery to 90,000 or 150,000 volts. Stun guns are non-lethal because their amperage is very low (no more than .6 amps.) However, they provide quite a punch! A one second contact with the assailant will knock him down. Five seconds will keep him down for approximately fifteen minutes. To stop an assailant with a stun gun, you need to make direct contact—you ram the stun gun into the person. It goes through clothing, even leather jackets. If the assailant grabs you while you are discharging the stun gun into him, you will not get shocked because the electronic impulse does not go back into you. The newer stun guns are more powerful and contain more features than their 40,000 volt cousins of several years ago. For example, one model, a 150,000 volt stun gun has a safety trigger, so that you do not shock yourself. This particular stun gun has double shock plates. The double shock plates will incapacitate an assailant who tries to take the stun gun away from you while you are trying to use it on him. Stun guns can also be used as a psychological self-defense weapon. I had the opportunity to use the stun gun in this way one afternoon. I went to a matinee performance of a play. I was on my way back to my car when a man came up from behind and tried to attack me. I wheeled around, and all it took was one squeeze of the trigger—a crackling blue bolt of lightening crossed the test arc. The man fled. As with tear gas, check with your local law enforcement agency on the legalities of the possession and use of stun guns for self-defense in your state.

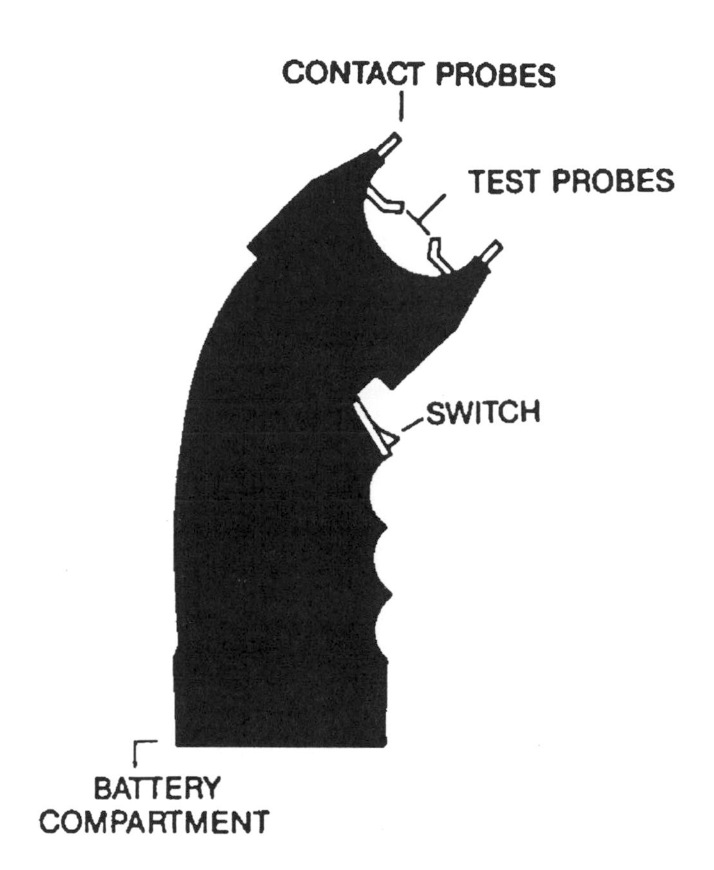

Figure 3. Stun Gun

Personal Alarms

A number of sound-producing devices are on the market, claiming to protect women from would-be muggers and rapists. These alarms range from old fashioned whistles, to air compressor driven shriek alarms, to battery powered multi-purpose portable alarms, to personal safety sirens. Prices for these devices range from a few dollars up to over one hundred dollars, depending upon the level of sophistication or complexity.

Do they work? Loud noise can be a deterrent. In Chapter 4—Rape Avoidance and Defense Strategies, the research into rape avoidance and resistance found that yelling fit into effective, active resistance strategies. Yet, Pauline Bart found that the most effective strategy was a combination of yelling and physical resistance.[111] Lila Furby and Baruch Fischhoff, who reviewed 24 studies of the effectiveness of self-defense strategies concurred. They found three strategies, when used as multiple strategies, worked the best: yelling, resistance with physical force, and fleeing/running. [112] I would not rely on a sound producing device, in and of itself, for self-defense. I choose to carry a non-lethal weapon, such as a stun gun or tear gas, over a personal alarm. A personal alarm can be used as part of a self-defense program, but is no substitute for knowledge and training in preventive psychological and physical defense skills.

How to Choose a Self-Defense Class

Co-ed Class or Self-Defense for Women Class?

This is a tough question. If you choose a co-ed class, then you will have both men and women to practice with. This is probably the biggest advantage. The energy is different though. When I teach a class which is strictly for women, many times bonding takes place between the women, and very special feelings of strength and self-esteem evolve. Women feel freer to share experiences and to develop an exalting sense of freedom, determination, and personal power.

What Should the Class Include?

Self-defense in general, and self-defense for women in particular, must include both psychological and physical skills. A class which only includes physical skills, or which places greater emphasis on physical skills than on psychological skills, does a disservice to the student. So far as I am concerned, a course in self-defense for women is a course in empowerment. My main goals in teaching self-defense for women are to empower women psychologically and to teach the skills so that they learn to protect themselves physically.

How to Select an Instructor

Check out the instructor's qualifications and philosophy to make sure that you are satisfied that she/he has the background, experience, and the same goals as you do for your class. Ask how the class will be conducted and what topics will be covered. You might also wish to ask to observe a class before you enroll. Be sure that the instructor is emphatic as to the issue of rape defense because self-defense for women is also self-defense against rape.

Remember, you as a woman do need to learn how to fight physically in order to fight back successfully. Always keep in mind that *it is not the size of the cat in the fight, but the size of the fight in the cat!*

TEN

THE MYTH EXPLODED

THE MYTH EXPLODED

The Myth Exploded

In Chapter 1—Exploding the Myth of Self-Defense, I asked the question, "What is this myth of self-defense?" The myth that self-defense should focus on forces external to ourselves (the assailant, the society, etc.) has been thoroughly discredited. From the many stories of empowerment and success and from the knowledge, options, and skills imparted to you in these chapters, you have the ability to conquer your real enemy—internal oppression and fear—and embrace your own inner strength.

Putting It All Together—A Vision for the Future

On the last day of class in my self-defense for women classes, we have a discussion—each student talks about what she has gained in the class and about how she feels now compared to the first day of class. Strength, confidence, self-esteem, new knowledge, changing of her life for the better, empowerment, a victim mentality replaced with a sense of power and strength from within: these are words and phrases frequently used to express new feelings and attitudes. A woman named Bonnie said, "I took a quantum leap in opening up to the dangers of the real world. I gave myself the precious gift of my freedom and independence. I am a free person; practicing awareness and being prepared mentally as well as physically keeps me from getting picked as a victim."

Margo, a woman who recently attended one of my self-defense for women classes, expressed to me that the experience had influenced her to make changes in her life. I asked her to write a statement. Her written account of her journey toward change exemplifies how for herself, and for other women, Margo has exploded the myth of self-defense.

"When I first heard that I would have the opportunity to take a self-defense class for women, I was thrilled to say the least. My job...kept me out on many a deserted street early in the morning, and the knowledge that I would learn skills to protect myself in potentially threatening situations was an added attribute to my ever growing need for self-worth and self-confidence. ...

"Upon entering the gymnasium where the class would be held, I was truly happy to see so many women of all ages present, as eager as I was to gain self-control over their lives and decrease the fear of being alone without a way to protect themselves. Judith Fein, the instructor, was herself a black belt in Korean karate and I was impressed with her command of the subject—but more than this there was a special aura about her that spoke more than just the learned skills—an air of integrity and confidence that immediately touched me someplace deep inside, much deeper than just words for the ears.

"As I listened to the lecture that first night and on the Wednesday nights that followed, I found an actual transformation of thought beginning to grow within myself as well. Yes, I learned the physical skills necessary to protect myself if attacked by an assailant, but even more important to me at this point in my life, I gained a new understanding for how vital and important is one's mental, spiritual and psychological outlook.

"For years I have been subject to psychological abuse—at the whim of whatever partner I chose to seemingly share my life with. Although I have a strong, independent nature, when I attached myself to another, I would always loose myself—who I was, everything that made me special, and would become submissive to his idea of what I should be and do instead of maintaining my own sense of my identity. At the point I entered the class, I felt like a woman in transition, desperately trying to forge my own sense of myself but seeming to fail miserably as often or more times than I succeeded. I seemed in danger of giving up and succumbing to a sense of oblivion—the victim of intense psychological abuse that daily drained me of any feeling of self-worth, independence or self-appreciation. I allowed my partner to intimidate me on every level and was in danger of relinquishing all the activities I did outside home and family that made me special, that made me me.

"As I listened to Judith's words, many times tears would come to my eyes and I realized what a triumph and godsend just being in that very class was for me. I became empowered by the group of women that bonded together to learn from this very special instructor who powerfully instilled us with the knowledge and confidence that we could take command of our lives—that we could refuse to let anyone intimidate us. Although she addressed all the skills we would need to protect ourselves, and these are certainly invaluable, what came across to me and pierced right to my thirsty mind was the control psychologically that was essential to maintain and exude in order to put an assailant in his place—be that threat physical or psychological.

"This class and its gifted instructor changed my life—planted a seed that I am now nurturing and refuse to let die no matter what the odds. I learned that *you have a choice of surrendering or resisting.* This knowledge is the tool I need in confrontation. I do have a choice. If someone is harassing or intimidating you—you have a choice—you do not need to be a helpless victim. You do not have to surrender to their control. And the most important tool I learned is *refuse to be intimidated.* I have lived for years with a 'victim mentality.' From Judith I learned I can *change the rules.* I don't have to be a victim. I understood how I sent out signals through my body language, my facial expression and behavior that threw my power away and enabled my psychological assailant to violate my space mentally and physically, and deprive me of my sense of worth. I learned that *if you are a powerful person things are done because of choice.* And the way to retain that power is through self-respect. *Self-defense begins with self-respect!* It became apparent to me that I was being manipulated by my partner placing constant guilt trips on anything I did just for me—and that I needed to trust my *gut feeling* on what was acceptable to me in order to stay in control and refuse to be manipulated or intimidated.

"As I heard these words, the tears began to flow. *Don't let anyone hurt you—respect yourself, believe in yourself, love yourself. Keep your power—don't give it away to anyone. Believe in your own power and communicate* <u>*that!*</u> *Maintain control of the situation—people respect you if you respect yourself—if you put yourself down, you are the victim, you get stepped on, get targeted. Maintain your own self-esteem, your own sense of power—trust your gut feeling and make sure you are not under someone else's control.*

"Although I knew Judith was speaking to everyone, I felt as though she was talking just to me, and I took every word, every emotion, every feeling right down into my very soul.

"During the six weeks I came to this class, I always came away with a tremendous sense of being uplifted, that no matter what, I could do it, I could change my life for the better.

"After one particularly bad session at home, of feeling severely battered, I came to class extremely forlorn—feeling as though I had failed. I had wanted so desperately to stand up for myself, be strong, and demonstrate all I had learned but once again had fallen prey to patterns well established for many years. But Judith helped pick me up by my bootstraps and made me realize *the only person that fails is someone who gives up!* I then realized, no matter how many times you get knocked down, <u>pick yourself up</u>, dust yourself off and keep going! Try again, and again, and again—don't give up. I saw the power and conviction in her face and eyes as she said *you can do whatever you want to do and be want you want to be. Don't accept anyone putting you down! Keep your power—don't give it to anyone!*

"I know now that I'll never give up no matter how long it takes or how tough the choice. My feeling of self-respect and confidence continues to grow and although at times the way is very scary and seems treacherous, I know the view from the top will be glorious and that I will get there. Believe in your integrity as a human being. Once you are powerful, you make choices, you do what you need to do!

"The valuable lessons I learned in this class will be with me forever. They are mine and no one can ever take them away for they have become a special part of me that I treasure as much as life itself. I know I still have a long way to go, but I am encouraged by the recent progress I have made, and the friends and teachers I have met along the way. Defining yourself and your sense of peace through a secure knowledge of your worth as an individual is a journey well worth taking. Don't let anyone knock you off that path for the rewards of this uphill climb are great and the feeling of wholeness and independence well worth the efforts needed to attain them."

Conquering The Enemy From Within

The enemy is our own fear and our own socialization. Through inward change, and the utilization of the tools of empowerment, we can and will overcome our fears and social conditioning. If rape is indeed an outward manifestation of our inward fears, when we conquer our own fears, we prevail. The threat of rape (and the overwhelming burden which accompanies it) which has interminably hung over women's heads, is lifted. We then feel free and in control of our lives. Truly amazing things can now happen, once we have the power of choice. Utilizing our self-esteem and new-found knowledge and abilities, we lift the lid off of the dark box of fear and step out into the light.

NOTES

1 The Press Democrat, April 24, 1992.
2 National Victim Resource Center, 1-800-627-6872.
3 Nancy Worthington, Artist's Statement.
4 Susan Faludi, Backlash, Crown Publishers, Inc., 1991, p. xxi.
5 Neely Tucker, "Youths' Views on Rape, Relationships," Knight-Ridder Newspapers, The Press Democrat, June 16, 1992.
6 James O. Whittaker, Introduction To Psychology, W. B. Saunders Co., 1965, p. 258.
7 Fanny Flagg, Fried Green Tomatoes at the Whistle Stop Cafe, McGraw-Hill, 1988.
8 Frank Pittman, "Beyond The BS and The Drumbeating," Psychology Today, February, 1992.
9 U.S. Department of Justice, Office of Justice Programs, Bureau of Justice Statistics, Violent Crime in the United States, March 1991.
10 James Selkin, "Behavioral Analysis of Rape," unpublished research report, Violence Research Unit, Denver General Hospital, p. 3.
11 Flagg in Fried Green Tomatoes at the Whislte Stop Cafe.
12 Pauline Bart, Stopping Rape, Pergamon Press, 1985, p. 113.
13 Susan Brownmiller, Against Our Will, Simon & Schuster, 1975.
14 Andra Media and Kathleen Thompson, Against Rape, Noonday, 1974.
15 James Selkin, Psychology Today, January, 1975.
16 James Selkin, "Protecting Personal Space: Victim and Resister Reactions to Assaultive Rape," Journal of Community Psychology, 1978, No. 6, pp. 263-268.
17 Ibid., p. 267.
18 Bart in Stopping Rape.
19 Ibid., pp. 108-112.
20 Ibid., pp. 41-42.
21 Lita Furby and Baruch Fischhoff. "Rape Self-Defense Strategies: A Review of Their Effectiveness," Victimology, in press.
22 Ibid., p. 36.
23 Furby & Fischhoff in Victimology, p.41.

24 Ibid., p. 39.
25 Ibid., p. 39.
26 Ibid., p. 40.
27 Pauline Bart, Avoiding Rape: A Comparative Study, Interna tional Sociological Association, Uppsala, Sweden, August, 1978, p. 9.
28 Ibid., p. 9.
29 Furby & Fischhoff in Victimology.
30 Joyce Levine-Macombie and Mary P. Koss, "Acquaintance Rape: Effective Avoidance Strategies," Psychology of Women Quarterly, 1986, Vol. 10, pp. 311-320.
31 Valerie Frankel, "Why Rape Statistics Don't Add Up," Mademoiselle Magazine, December, 1991.
32 Mary Koss, et al., "The Scope of Rape: Incidence and Prevalence of Sexual Agression and Victimization in a National Sample of Higher Education Students," Journal of Consulting and Clinical Psychology, 1987, Vol. 55, No. 2, pp. 162-170.
33 U.S. Department of Justice, "Crime in the United States," Uniform Crime Reports, 1990.
34 San Francisco State University, Sexual Assault Policy, May, 1991.
35 Valerie Frankel in "Why Rape Statistics Don't Add Up,"
36 "1 in 8 U.S. Women Raped," Press Democrat, April 24, 1992.
37 U.S. Department of Justice, Criminal Victimization in the United States, 1990.
38 "1 in 8 U.S. Women Raped," Press Democrat, April 24, 1992.
39 Valerie Frankel in "Why Rape Statistics Don't Add Up."
40 Ibid.
41 Neely Tucker, "Youths' Views on Rape, Relationships, " Knight-Ridder Newspapers, June 16, 1992.
42 Subcommittee on Domestic and International Scientific Planning, Analysis and Cooperation, Research into Violent Behavior: Overview and Sexual Assaults, U.S. Government Printing Office, 1978.
43 Bonny Saludes, "Trial Ordered For Three in Rape of 17-Year Old," The Press Democrat, September 16, 1992.
44 Le Aanne Schreiber, "Campus Rape," Glamour Magazine, September 1990.
45 Ibid.
46 John Marcus, "Campus Crime Statistics Come To Light," Associated Press, September 13, 1991.
47 Ibid.

48 San Francisco State University, Sexual Assault Policy, May 1991.
49 Jill Neimark, "Out of Bounds: The Truth About Athletes and Rape," Mademoiselle, May 1991.
50 Valerie Frankel, "Life After Rape," Mademoiselle, May, 1991.
51 Jill Neimark in Mademoiselle.
52 Ibid.
53 Ibid.
54 Associated Press, September 9, 1992.
55 Jill Neimark in Mademoiselle.
56 Susan Smith, Fear or Freedom, Mother Courage Press, 1986, pp. 32-33.
57 Carla Marinucci, "Woman Soldier Harassed to Dealth?", San Francisco Examiner, Sept. 13, 1992.
58 ABC, Primetime Live, October 1, 1992.
59 Ellen Goodman, "Forcing the Navy to Change," Press Democrat, September 29, 1992.
60 Ibid.
61 Captain Judith Fein, "Letter of Resignation," U.S. Army, 1977.
62 HQ Eighth U.S. Army, "Subject: Abuse of APO Priviledges," Department of the Army, November 6, 1968. "
63 Headquarters, Republic of Korea Army Securiy Command, "Subject: Letter of Appreciation," November30, 1968.
64 Ellyn E. Spagins, Ed., "The Cost of Sexual Harassment," Inc. Magazine, May 1992.
65 Benjamin Rifkin, Art History, College Notes Inc., 1963, p. 10.
66 Faludi, in Backlash, p. 369.
67 Ibid., p. 393.
68 Gloria Steinem, Revolution From Within, Little, Brown and Company, 1992.
69 Ibid., p. 187.
70 Susan Swartz, "Barbie's still a doll, but she's no role model", The Press Democrat, October 25, 1992.
71 Anonymous.
72 Susan Strauss, Sexual Harassment and Teens, Free Spirit Publishing, Inc., 1992.
73 Inc. Magazine, August 1992, p. 16.
74 Ronni Sandroff, "Sexual Harassment, The Inside Story," Working Woman Magazine, June 1992, p. 47.

75 Ibid., p. 48.
76 The California Labor Letter, "Sexual Harassment in the Work place," Vol. II, No. 11, November 1991.
77 Deborah Jacobs, "Don't let sexual harassment ruin a job you otherwise enjoy," National Business Employment Weekly, Spring 1992.
78 Inc. Magazine, August 1992, p. 16.
79 Edward Markim, "The Man With The Hoe."
80 U.S. Department of Justice. "Uniform Crime Reports, 1987," Crime in the United States, 1988, p. 6.
81 Press Democrat, April 24, 1992.
82 Ibid.
83 Susan Faludi in Backlash.
84 Elizabeth Kuster, "Don't 'hey, baby' Me," Glamour, September 1992.
85 Ibid.
86 Kiley Armstrong, "Violence victimizes car drivers," Associated Press, November 10, 1992.
87 Ibid.
88 Pame Roscoe, Statement, May 10, 1992.
89 Kihak Henry Cho, Korean Karate, Charles E. Tuttle Company, 1968, p. 22.
90 Ibid.
91 Ibid, p. 46
92 Greg Cahill, "Women and Guns," Pacific Sun, February 16, 1990.
93 Violent Crime in the United States, p. 3.
94 Ibid.
95 Handgun Control, Inc., Briefing Book, September 18, 1989.
96 Sarah Lavender Smith, "Women and Guns," The Paper, July 16, 1992.
97 Ibid.
98 Ibid.
99 Ibid.
100 San Francisco Chronicle, August 18, 1989.
101 Sarah Lavender Smith in "Women and Guns."
102 Ibid.
103 Ibid.
104 Ibid.
105 Ibid.

106 Ibid.
107 Arthur L. Kellermann, M.D., M.P.H. and Donald T. Reay, M.D. "Protection or Peril? An Analysis of Firearm-Related Deaths in the Home," The New England Journal of Medicine, Vol. 314, No. 24, June 12, 1986.
108 "Facts about Children and Handguns," The Center to Prevent Handgun Violence, February, 1991.
109 "Facts about Teen Suicide and Handguns," The Center to Prevent Handgun Violence, February, 1991.
110 Chief J.P. Morgan, "Oleoresin Capsicum Policy Considerations," The Police Chief, August, 1992.
111 Pauline Bart, in Stopping Rape, p. 113.
112 Lita Furby and Baruch Fichhoff in Victimology.

INDEX

A

B

C

E

F

G

I

J

M

P

R

S

W